MASTERING ROCK KEYBOARD

National Keyboard Workshop Book
Approved Curriculum

Alfred, the leader in educational publishing, and the National Keyboard Workshop, one of America's finest contemporary music schools, have joined forces to bring you the best, most progressive educational tools possible. We hope you will enjoy this book and encourage you to look for other fine products from Alfred and the National Keyboard Workshop.

This book was acquired, edited and produced by Workshop Arts, Inc., the publishing arm of the National Guitar Workshop.
Nathaniel Gunod, editor
Joe Bouchard, music typesetter
Cathy Bolduc, design
CD recorded at Bar None Studios, Cheshire, CT
Cover photograph: Karen Miller

TABLE OF CONTENTS

00

Track 1

A compact disc is available for this book. This disc can make learning with the book easier and more enjoyable. This symbol will appear next to every example that is on the CD. Use the CD to help insure that you are capturing the feel of the examples, interpreting the rhythms correctly, and so on. The track numbers below the symbols correspond directly to the example you want to hear. Track 1 will help you tune your electronic keyboard to the CD. Have fun!

ABOUT THE AUTHOR

A classically trained pianist with the heart of a rocker, Sheila Romeo has a keen interest in everything from music by the great composers of centuries past, to rock, new age and classical music performed by the many talented artists of today. Sheila graduated *cum laude* from Berklee College of Music in 1992 where she studied keyboard and majored in Music Production & Engineering and Music Synthesis.

Sheila's classical background and love of rock music naturally translate to the genre of progressive rock. She has studied and played in the styles of Steve Walsh (Kansas), Rick Wakeman (Yes), Tony Banks (Genesis) and Keith Emerson (Emerson, Lake and Palmer). She has played on many studio sessions and projects, as well as in several bands.

As an audio engineer, Sheila worked at various recording studios in the Boston area, and oftentimes worked with major label artists, including Peter Wolf, Ami Mann and various rap and R&B artists on Island Records. She is currently residing in the New York City area where she writes, arranges and records at her home studio, occasionally playing on other studio sessions and working on various outside engineering projects.

INTRODUCTION

Hello, and welcome to *Mastering Rock Keyboard*. I hope you will enjoy studying the pieces in this book as much as I have enjoyed putting them together for you.

This is an advanced book. You will need to have completed either the two previous books in this series, *Beginning Rock Keyboard* and *Intermediate Rock Keyboard,* or know the following: how to read music; scales, arpeggios and modes in all keys; what a synthesizer is and how to call up different sounds. Therefore, you should have at least a few years of serious playing behind you and some experience with soloing.

Because progressive rock keyboardists play such a featured role in their bands, they get the greatest workout. That is why we will be studying many of the techniques from that style.

The goal is for you to have fun while getting a sense of the history of rock 'n' roll. I hope you will also get a feel for the rhyme and reason behind why music "works." If you can get through this book, you will be able to play out in any rock keyboard situation. Just practice as much as you can, listen to and play along with the music referenced and always use a metronome.

There is a quick review of some basic music principles at the front of the book. Flip through it and, if it seems elementary, turn to Chapter 2 and dig in.

Now, let's get started!

ACKNOWLEDGEMENTS

Thank you to all the people at the National Guitar and Keyboard Workshop and Alfred Publishing for making this project possible, especially Nat Gunod for giving me a shot at this, Joe Bouchard for all of the endless hours he spent engraving and editing my manuscripts and Cathy Bolduc for making everything fit beautifully onto the pages. I would also like to thank my piano teacher of many years, John Molnar, for teaching me practically everything I needed to know in order to write this book. A huge thanks goes to Terry Syrek (author of the *Shred is Not Dead* video), whose insight into progressive rock and improvisation was essential to this project. The very talented and artistic Tracey Munz gets a big thank you for all of the work she put into my photo. A great big, huge thank you to the band, three of the most talented musicians I've ever had the privilege of knowing: Terry Syrek (guitar); Greg Kalember (drums); and Rob Fiorentino (bass). And lastly, thank you to my family and friends who, despite their better judgment, have supported all of my musical pursuits, especially this project.

CHAPTER 1

Music Review

MAJOR SCALES AND KEY SIGNATURES

The major scale is made up of eight notes which, when played in sequence, make the familiar melody: do, re, mi, fa, sol, la, ti, do.   The scale is constructed by starting on any note and following this pattern of whole step and half step intervals:

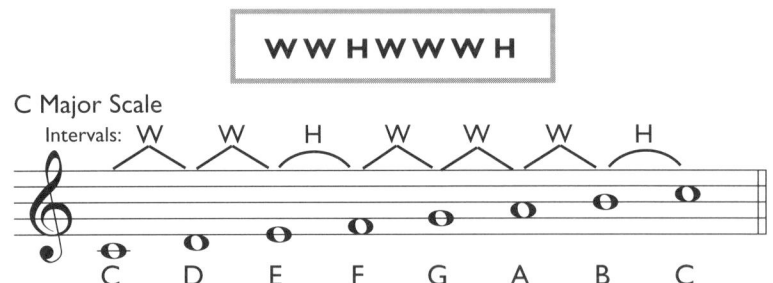

W = Whole step
H = Half step

In order to keep the pattern, each scale has its own combination of flats or sharps. On a keyboard, this means each major scale has a different arrangement of black and white keys.

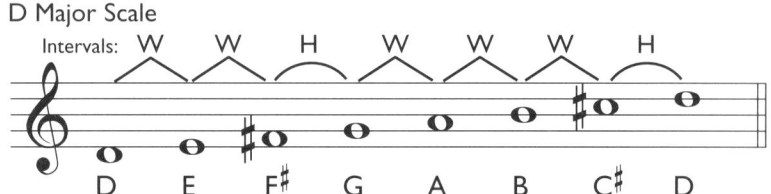

The *key signature* contains the flats or sharps specific to a major scale. The name of the key is the same as the note the scale started from, which we call the *root*.

Here are the key signatures for all the major keys:

FINGERINGS FOR MAJOR SCALES

The *fingering* (order of the fingers used) for each scale depends on its pattern of white and black notes. Here are the easiest fingerings for each major scale:

INTERVALS

All of the different intervals we use in music have numeric names. For instance, another name for a half step is a *minor second*. This may also be called a *flat second* and written as ♭2.

Two half steps together equal one *whole step*, also called a *major second*, and written as 2.

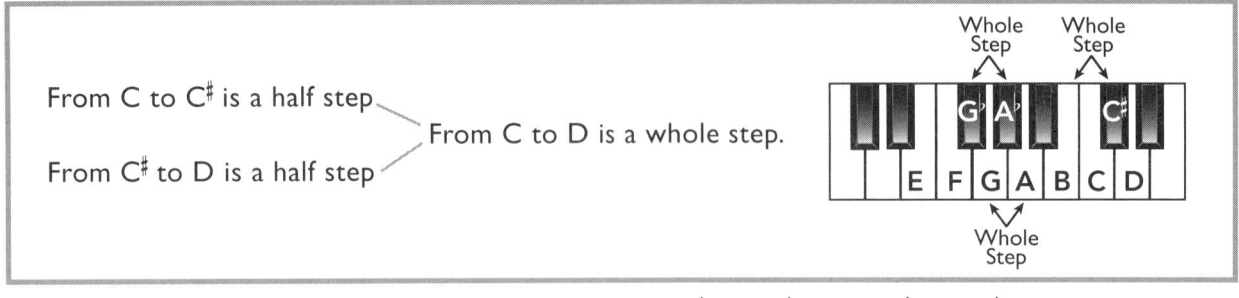

From C to C♯ is a half step.
From C♯ to D is a half step.

From C to D is a whole step.

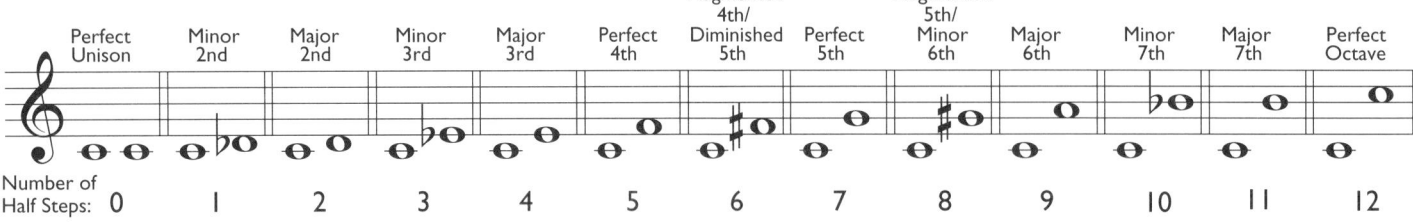

Number of Half Steps: 0 1 2 3 4 5 6 7 8 9 10 11 12

There are twelve half steps in an *octave*. An octave is the distance between the two closest notes with the same name.

THE INTERVALS IN AN OCTAVE

Number	Number of Half Steps	Interval	Abbreviation
1	0	perfect unison	PU
♭2	1	minor 2nd	min2
2	2	major 2nd	Maj2
♭3	3	minor 3rd	min3
3	4	major 3rd	Maj3
4	5	perfect 4th	P4
♯4	6 ("tritone")	augmented 4th	Aug4
♭5	6 ("tritone")	diminished 5th	dim5
5	7	perfect 5th	P5
♯5	8	augmented 5th	Aug5
♭6	8	minor 6th	min6
6	9	major 6th	Maj6
♭7	10	minor 7th	min7
7	11	major 7th	Maj7
1	12	perfect octave	P8

INTERVAL INVERSION

Intervals in music are often inverted—turned upside-down. The total number of half steps in any interval plus its inversion add up to one octave (twelve half steps). In addition, the quality of the interval changes except for perfect intervals: major becomes minor; minor becomes major; diminished becomes augmented; augmented becomes diminished; perfect remains perfect.

For example: The inversion of a major 3rd(four half steps) = a minor 6th (eight half steps).

CYCLE OF 5THS

Notice that the major scales on page 7 moved from key to key at an interval of a perfect 5th each time a sharp or flat was added to the key signature. For the sharp keys, we moved up in 5ths. For flat keys, we moved down in 5ths. In addition, each new sharp note added to the key signature was a perfect 5th above the last one, and each new flat note added was a perfect 5th below the last one. This movement is called the *cycle of 5ths*. The cycle of 5ths forms the basis for most harmonic movement in popular music.

Since an inverted perfect 5th is a perfect 4th, the cycle of 5ths is sometimes called the cycle of 4ths. It's the same thing.

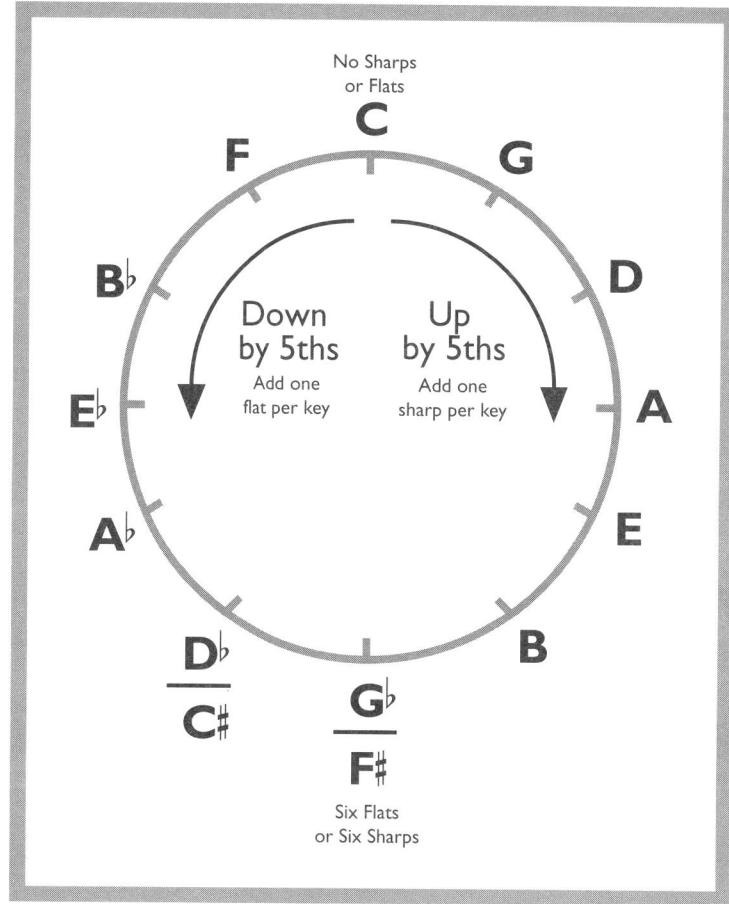

SWING FEEL

To understand the swing feel, we need to look at the *triplet*. When we divide the quarter-note beat in two, we get eighth notes. When we divide an eighth note in two, we get sixteenth notes. With triplets, we divide the quarter-note beat into three eighth notes. We can count "one-and-a, two-and-a, three . . ." to keep track of the beat.

Lots of blues-influenced rock is notated with *swing eighth notes*. A pair of swing eighths sounds like a triplet with the first two notes tied together (a tie makes the first note last as long as both tied notes combined, without playing the second note).

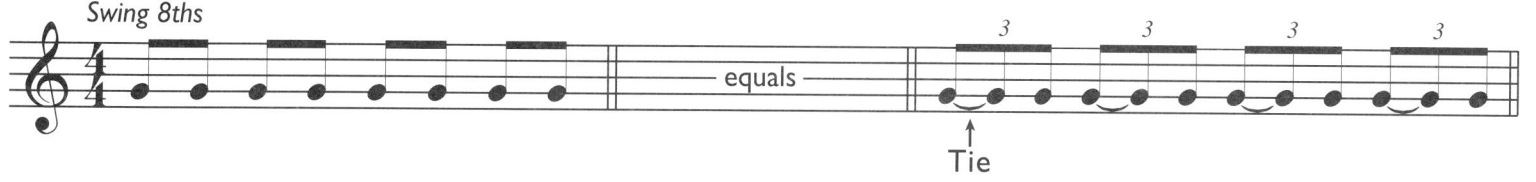

Let's look at what happens if we play all the notes found in the C Major scale, but start on the note A. The scale now has a very different sound because it has become a minor scale—A Minor. The key signature for A Minor is the same as the key signature for C Major. There are no sharps or flats in it. For each major key, there is a *relative minor key* which shares the same key signature.

The relative minor key's root is the 6th degree, or note, of the major scale.

For example, in the key of C Major, the 6th degree of the scale is A:

C	D	E	F	G	A	B
1	2	3	4	5	6	7

So, the relative minor to C Major is A Minor and the scale, called the *natural minor scale,* contains the same notes but in a different order:

A	B	C	D	E	F	G
1	2	3	4	5	6	7

The pattern of half steps and whole steps for the natural minor scale is:

W	H	W	W	H	W	W

C NATURAL MINOR

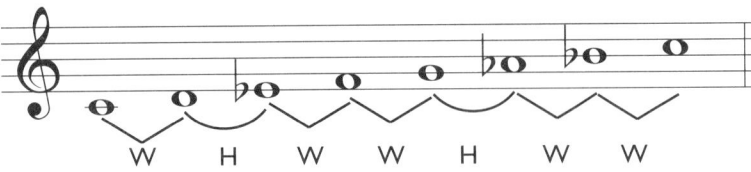

W   H   W   W   H   W   W

Look at the cycle of 5ths again. The major key cycle is on the inside. The relative minor for each major key is outside the circle. Just like the major keys, the minor keys move up in 5ths as you add sharps, and down in 5ths as you add flats to the key signature.

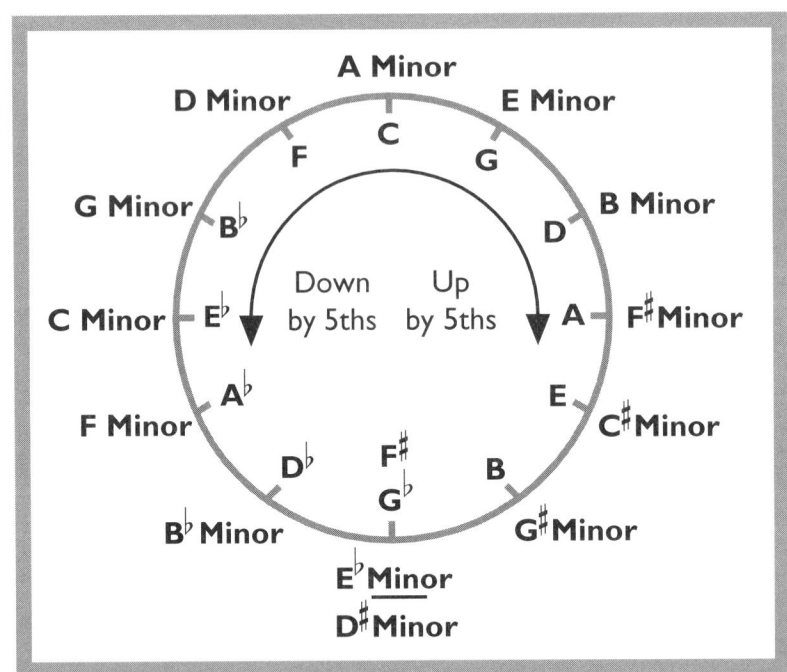

FINGERINGS FOR NATURAL MINOR SCALES

The chart below shows the notes and best fingerings for the twelve natural minor scales:

THE MAJOR PENTATONIC SCALE

The major and minor pentatonic scales are very important to rock improvisation. These scales get the name "pentatonic" from the fact that they are five-note scales. ("Penta" is the Greek word for "five.") The major and natural minor scales are eight-note scales.

Here is the "formula" for the major pentatonic scale, along with the corresponding notes in the key of C:

1	2	3	5	6
C	D	E	G	A

The scale has a major sound because the 3rd, E, is a major 3rd (four half steps above the root—see the interval chart on page 8).

The best way to practice pentatonic scales on the keyboard is to play them over three octaves using the fingerings below that repeat every two octaves.

TWO-OCTAVE FINGERINGS FOR MAJOR PENTATONIC SCALES

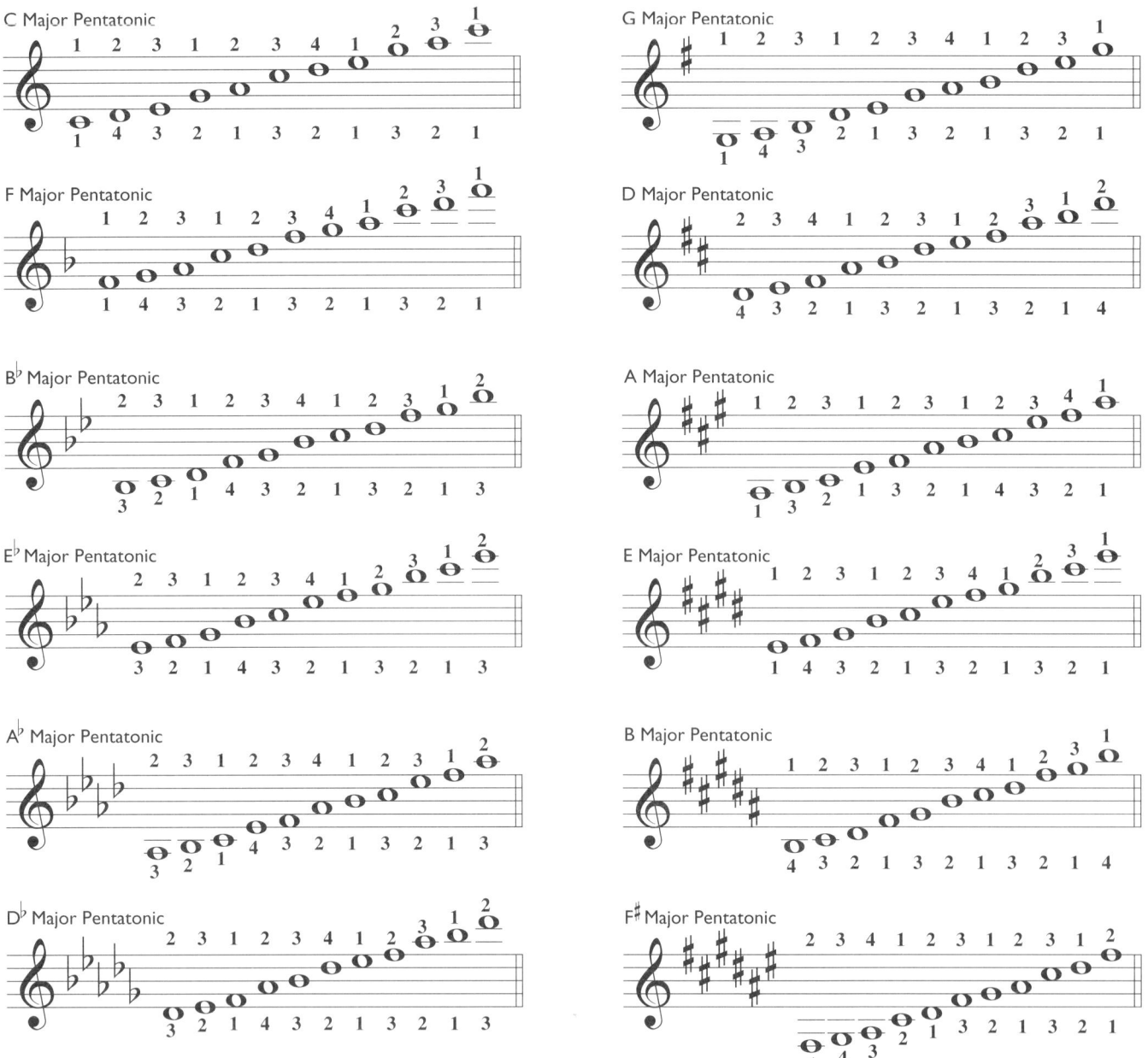

THE MINOR PENTATONIC SCALE

Just as for every major scale there is a relative minor scale (see page 10), for every major pentatonic scale there is a relative minor pentatonic scale. The root of the relative minor key is a major 6th above the root of the major key.

Major Pentatonic Formula:	1	2	3		5	6	1
C Major Pentatonic:	C	D	E		G	A	C
A Minor Pentatonic:				A	C	D	E	G	(A)

Numbering the notes of the minor pentatonic relative to its root gives us a new formula:

Minor Pentatonic Formula

A	C	D	E	G
1	♭3	4	5	♭7

The C Minor Pentatonic scale contains two blue notes for the key of C: E♭ and B♭. These notes are not in the key of C and they give a bluesy character to a solo—hence the name "blue notes." It also contains chord tones from all three triads used in a C blues progression (C, F, G).

TWO-OCTAVE FINGERINGS FOR THE MINOR PENTATONIC SCALES

A Minor Pentatonic

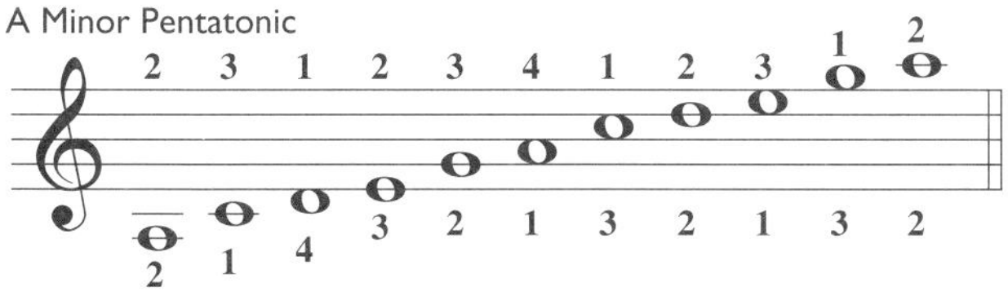

D Minor Pentatonic

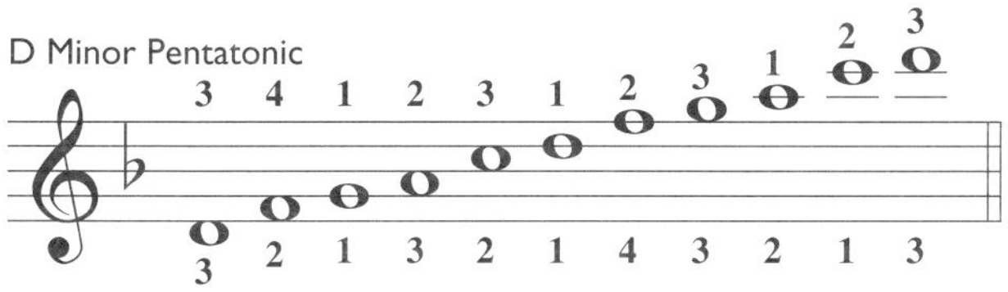

G Minor Pentatonic

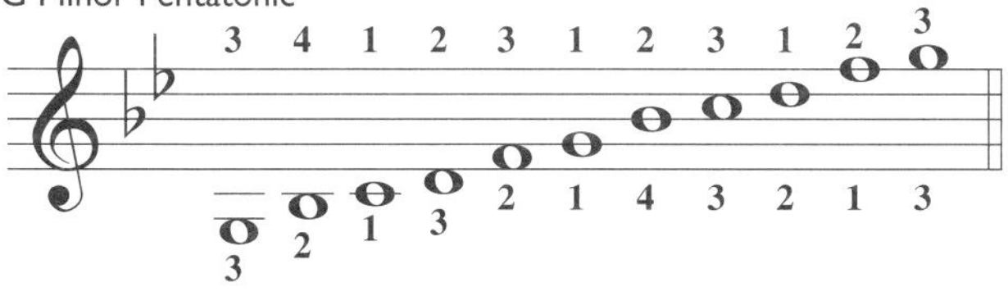

C Minor Pentatonic

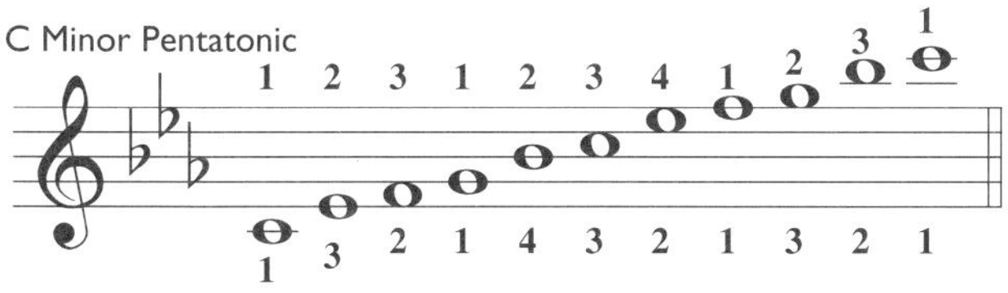

F Minor Pentatonic

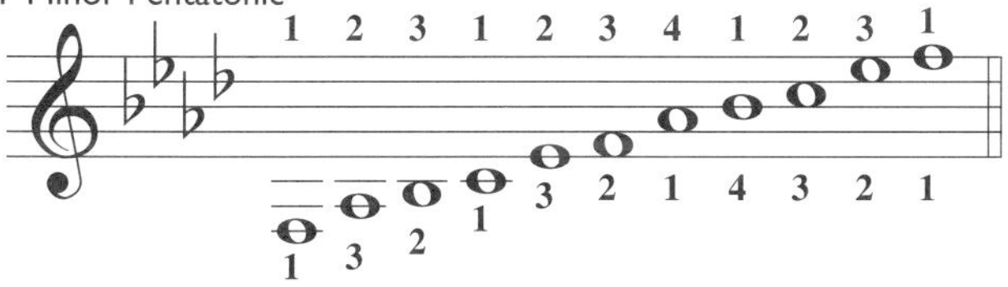

B♭ Minor Pentatonic

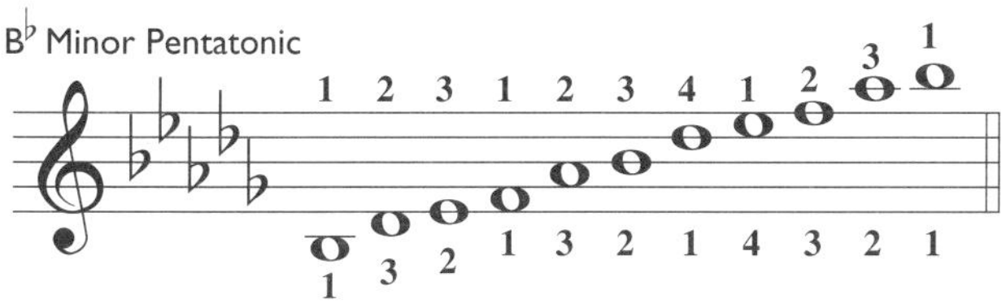

E Minor Pentatonic

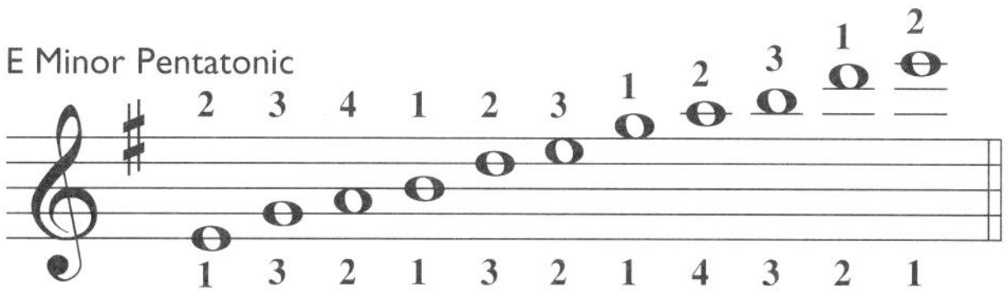

B Minor Pentatonic

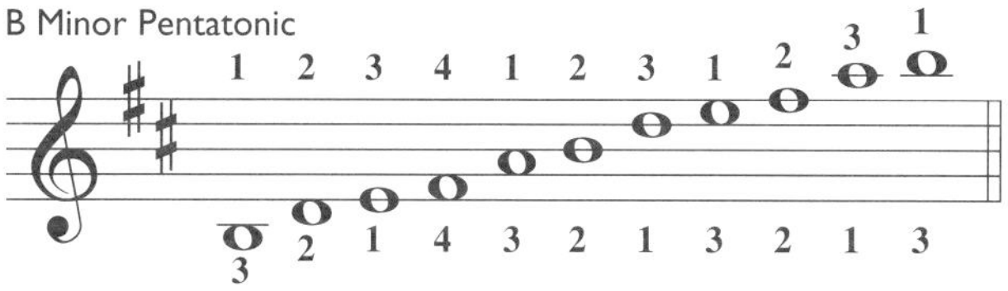

F♯ Minor Pentatonic

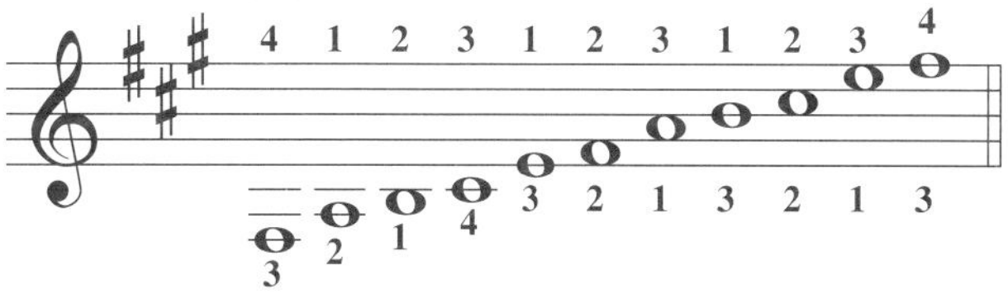

C♯ Minor Pentatonic

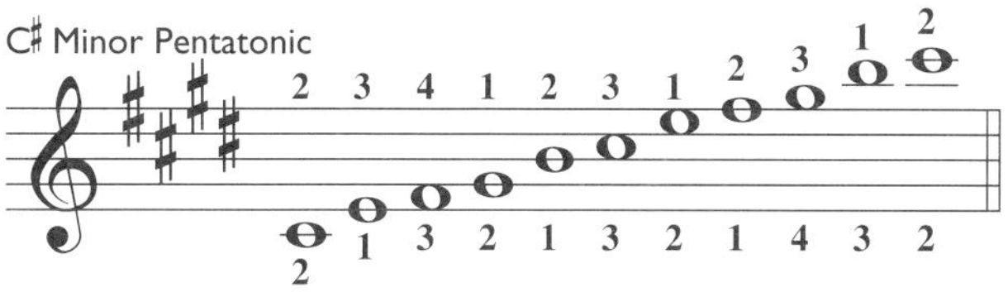

G♯ Minor Pentatonic

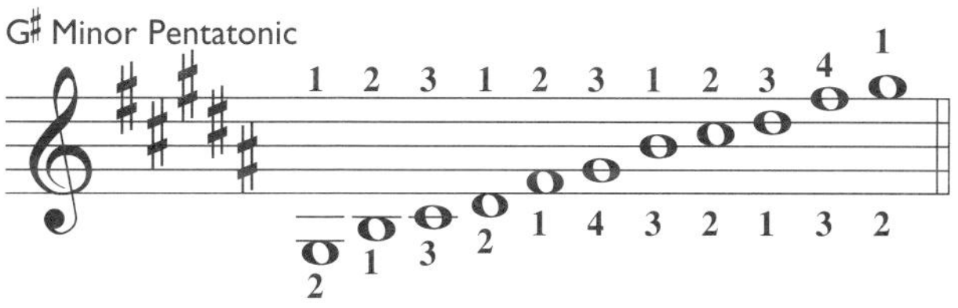

D♯ Minor Pentatonic

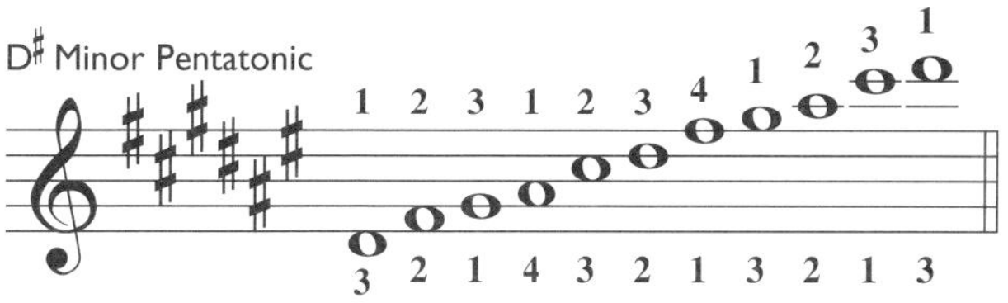

THE BLUES SCALE

We can make the minor pentatonic scale more colorful by adding one more note to it—the ♭5. This scale is often called *the blues scale*.

Here is the C Blues scale:

The Formula:	1	♭3	4	♭5	5	♭7
In C:	C	E♭	F	G♭	G	B♭

Since it includes three blue notes, ♭3, ♭5 and ♭7, this scale is going to provide you with a lot of great blues-influenced sounds.

RIGHT-HAND FINGERINGS FOR THE BLUES SCALE IN TWELVE KEYS

Since the blues scale contains six notes, each one-octave fingering has either two groups of three (for example, 1-2-3, 1-2-3) or a group of two and a group of four (for example, 1-2, 1-2-3-4).

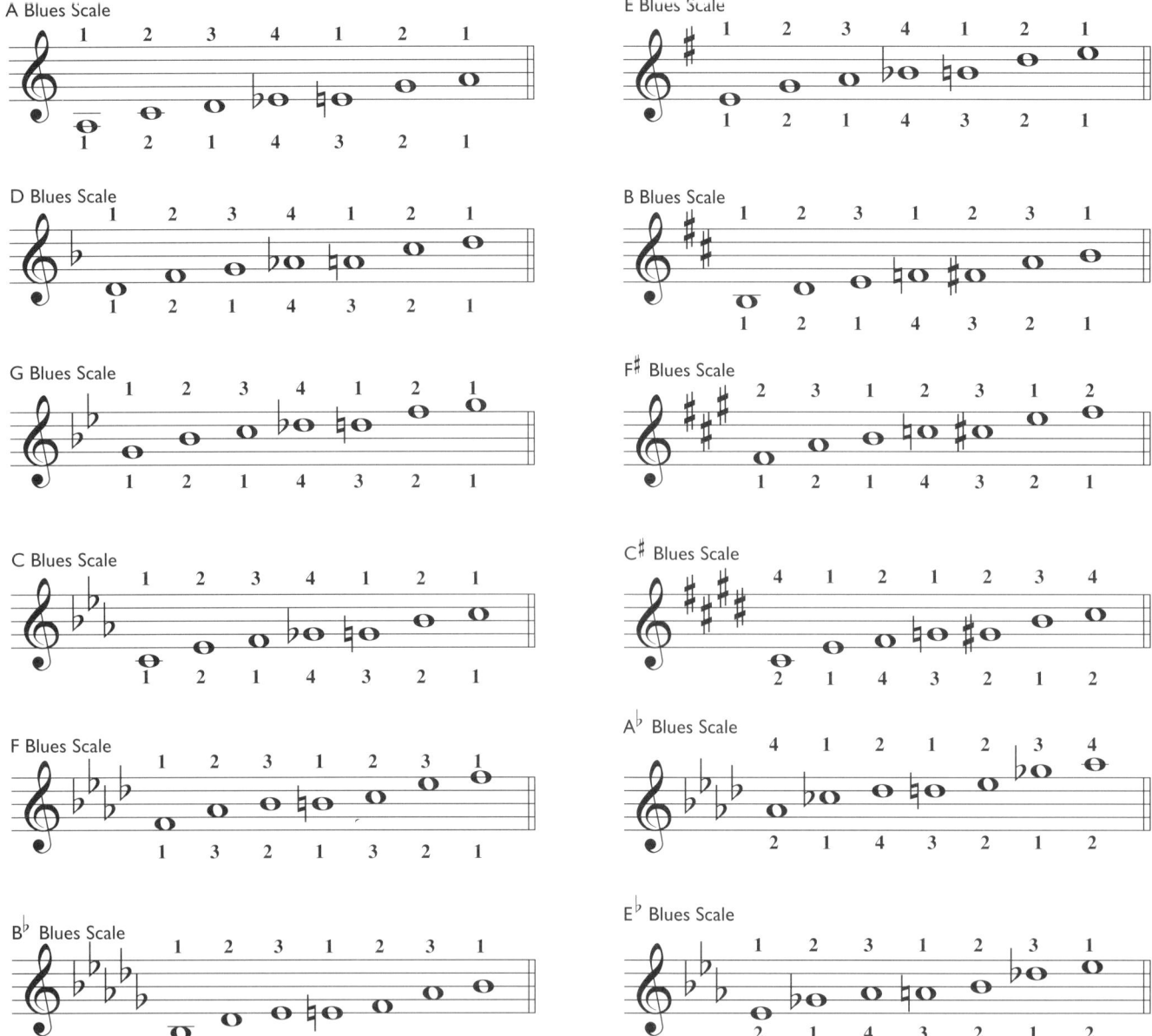

TRIADS

Triads are made by stacking two intervals of a third (major 3rds or minor 3rds).

You can build a major triad by taking the root (1), 3rd (3) and 5th (5) of the major scale.

In the key of C Major, for example, the root, 3rd and 5th are C, E and G. Together, these notes form a C Major triad (C).

 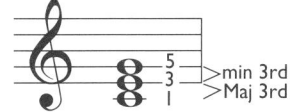

From C to E is a major 3rd (four half steps).
From E to G is a minor 3rd (three half steps).
A major triad is made up of a major 3rd with a minor 3rd above it.

Let's lower the 3rd, E, by a half step so we have C, E♭ and G. We now have the root, 3rd and 5th of the C Natural Minor scale. Together, these notes form a C Minor triad (Cmin).

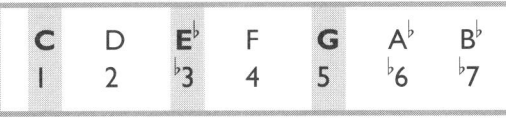 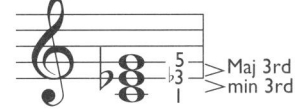

From C to E♭ is a minor 3rd.
From E♭ to G is a major 3rd.
A minor triad is made up of a minor 3rd with a major 3rd above it.

There are two other types of triads which we will encounter less frequently:

Diminished triad (dim) — A minor triad with a lowered 5th. For example: C, E♭, G♭ is Cdim or C°.
Augmented triad (Aug) — A major triad with a raised 5th. For example: C, E, G♯ is CAug.

Ray Manzarek's first hit record was Light My Fire *with the Doors in 1967. The album version featured an extended combo organ solo.*

DIATONIC TRIADS

Diatonic means "of the key." *Diatonic triads* are triads found within the scale of a particular key.

Every major scale contains the following pattern of major, minor and diminished triads:

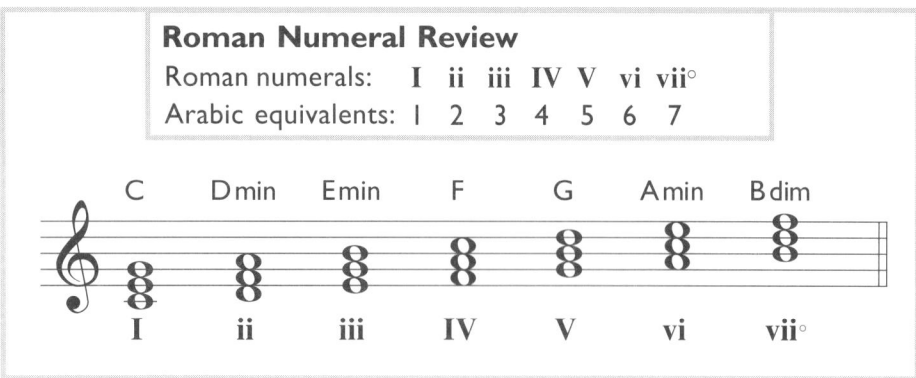

Roman Numeral Review
Roman numerals: I ii iii IV V vi vii°
Arabic equivalents: 1 2 3 4 5 6 7

We use Roman numerals to label the diatonic triads according to the degree of the scale they are built on. Upper case numerals indicate major triads. Lower case numerals indicate minor triads.

Let's take the key of C Major and build a triad on each degree of the scale using only notes found in the C Major scale.

C D E F G A B C

From the root, the notes are C, E and G—a C Major triad. This is the I chord.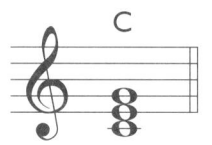

From the second note of the scale, the notes are D, F and A—a D Minor triad. This is the ii chord.

Continuing up the scale we'll get:

E Minor	iii
F Major	IV
G Major	V
A Minor	vi
B Diminished	vii°

The natural minor scale contains the following pattern of diatonic triads:

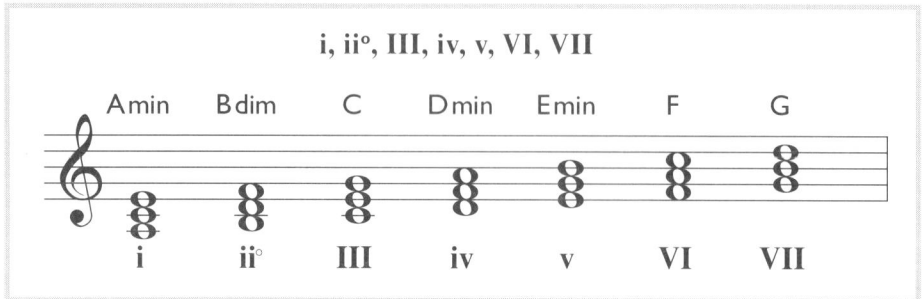

i, ii°, III, iv, v, VI, VII

For example, in the key of C Minor, the diatonic triads are:

C D E♭ F G A♭ B♭ C

C	Minor	i
D	Diminished	ii°
E♭	Major	III
F	Minor	iv
G	Minor	v
A♭	Major	VI
B♭	Major	VII

Exercise:
Starting with a G Major triad, play all the diatonic triads in the key of G Major. Notice whether each triad you play is major, minor or diminished. Did you get the correct pattern of triads for a major key?

7TH CHORDS

If we add one more 3rd to a triad, it becomes a 7th chord. Let's look at the notes of the C major scale again and this time, notice every other note:

C	D	E	F	G	A	B
1	2	3	4	5	6	7

We can use every other note of the scale to build a four-note chord:

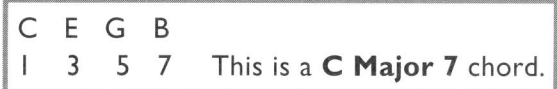

C	E	G	B	
1	3	5	7	This is a **C Major 7** chord.

To make a C Dominant 7th chord, or **C7**, we lower the 7th by a half step (♭7), from B to B♭.

C	E	G	B♭	
1	3	5	♭7	This is a **C7** chord.

Another way to understand dominant 7th chords is to build them from the major scale in which their root is the 5th degree. For example, C is the 5th degree of F Major. So build a C7 chord by taking every other note of the F Major scale starting on C.

Position in scale:	1	2	3	4	5	6	7	1	2	3	4
F Major scale:	F	G	A	B♭	C	D	E	F	G	A	B♭
C7 chord:					C			E		G	B♭
Position in chord:					1			3		5	♭7

Practice playing dominant 7th chords in root position around the cycle of 5ths. Play the root of each chord in your left hand.

Below are two other common kinds of 7th chords. The minor 7th has a ♭3 abd ♭7. The minor 7♭5 has a ♭3, ♭5 and ♭7.

C	E♭	G	B♭	
1	♭3	5	♭7	This is a **Cmin7** chord.

C	E♭	G♭	B♭	
1	♭3	♭5	♭7	This is a **Cmin7♭5** chord.

DIATONIC HARMONY WITH 7TH CHORDS

We build diatonic 7th chords in a key the same way we build diatonic triads. The only difference is that we stack an extra note on top.

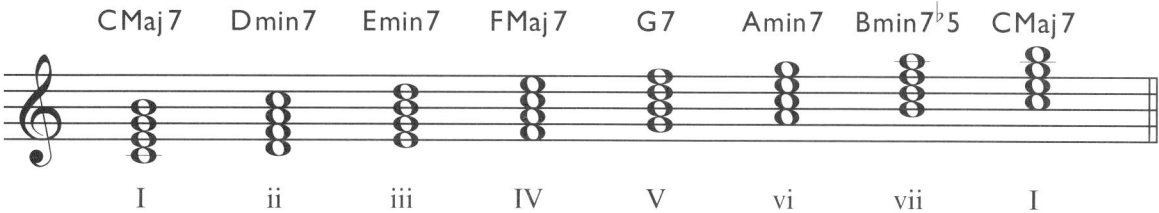

In every major key, the following diatonic 7th chords are built from each degree of the scale:

I	Maj7		V	Dominant 7
ii	min7		vi	min7
iii	min7		vii°	min7♭5
IV	Maj7			

CHORD EXTENSIONS

Adding extensions to chords makes them colorful. The complex-sounding numeric names make the topic seem tricky, but it's really very easy.

Let's say we're in C Major. We're on the 4th degree, F natural, and we want to form the triad built from that degree. So, we stack a couple 3rds and wind up with an F Major triad.

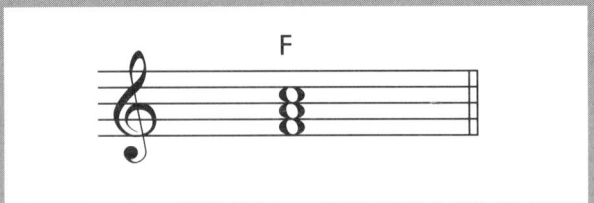

Then we decide that we want more color, so we look for the 7th chord built from the same degree. We take the triad we've already found and stack another 3rd on top of that, giving us FMaj7.

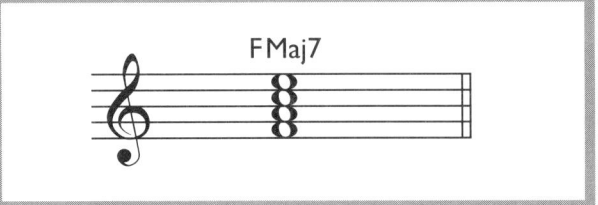

Since that sounds good, let's keep stacking more 3rds, alternating every other note until we repeat one. Now that's one big, fat, colorful chord.

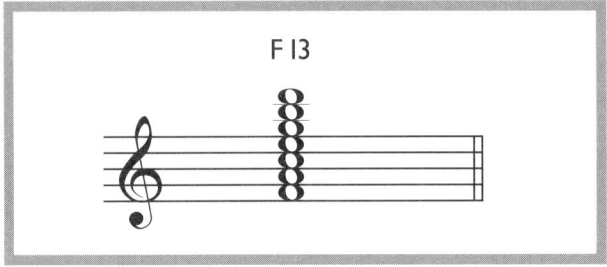

This is the basic concept behind *chord extensions*. The four notes that make up a 7th chord aren't the only notes that sound good when played with that chord.

Below is a two-octave C Major scale, labeled by scale degree. Since the new notes we are talking about are extensions, we need the second octave to distinguish them from the chord tones (which would be in the first octave).

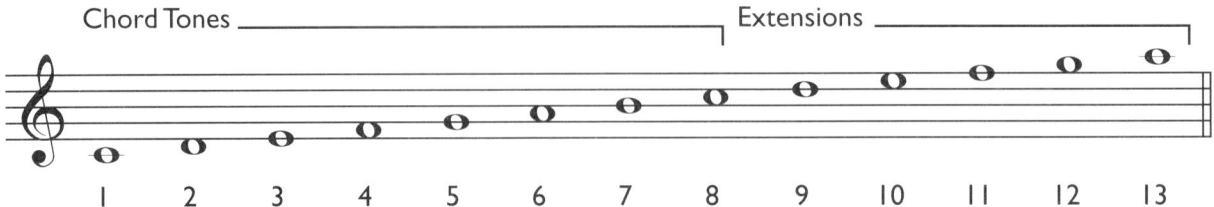

If we stack 3rds from C, we wind up with this voicing. The root, 3rd, 5th and 7th are there as usual with the addition of the 9th, 11th and 13th. 9ths, 11ths and 13ths are typically the extensions you will be dealing with. The others are simply repetitions of chord tones. The distinction is important; calling the D in this chord the 9th and not the 2nd indicates that it is an extension and not a fundamental part of the chord. In other words, extensions are always a higher number than 7.

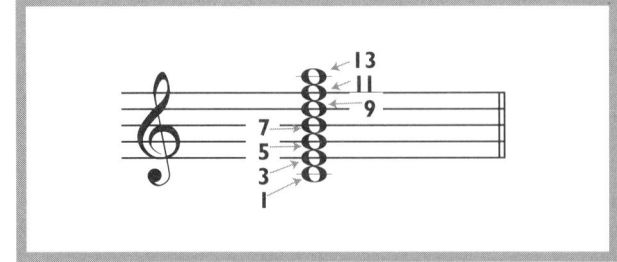

THE MODES OF THE MAJOR SCALE

In the last decade or two, much of the rock and jazz we have heard has been based less and less on traditional scales and more on *modal* scales.

Modes are re-orderings of a *parent scale*. If we take the notes of a C Major scale, and begin and end on a note other than C, we are playing a mode of the scale. The ancient Greeks believed the different modes would effect human psychology in particular ways and specific modes became part of many ceremonies and celebrations.

THE MODES OF THE MAJOR SCALE ARE:

Ionian:	built on the 1st degree. This is identical to the major scale.
Dorian:	built on the 2nd degree.
Phrygian:	built on the 3rd degree.
Lydian:	built on the 4th degree.
Mixolydian:	built on the 5th degree.
Aeolian:	built on the 6th degree. This is identical to the natural minor.
Locrian:	built on the 7th degree.

CHAPTER 2

Warming Up

As with anything that requires repetitive muscular movement, playing a musical instrument like the piano increases susceptibility to muscular injury, such as tendonitis. Just as an athlete warms up his or her muscles before beginning a workout, it is important to warm up before playing. A good way to do this is by playing scales and arpeggios.

SCALES

By now, you should know all of your scales as well as the fingerings for each key. Therefore, this book will cover different ways to use scales to appropriately warm up your muscles without getting bored.

Each day, pick a scale type. If you pick major, begin playing a C Major scale in the manner depicted below, then ascend up a half step to repeat the scale in the next key each time the pattern is completed. Do this until you have played all the scales.

Try to keep in mind that when practicing your scales, you are working on more than just warming up your muscles. You are also working on timing, technique and endurance. Always use a metronome and ONLY play as fast as you can control the sixteenth notes. Each time you master a tempo, adjust the metronome up a notch. This will greatly improve your ability to play in an ensemble situation. The more solid your rhythm, the easier and more natural it will be to lock into grooves with other musicians.

8va = *Ottava alta.* Play an octave higher than written.

Below is another way to warm up with scales. Again, pick a scale type and play through every key. In this case we'll use natural minor. The example below is in E♭ Natural Minor. This challenges the mind more than the previous exercise. The fingerings for some keys get tricky when the right and left hands are traveling in opposite directions. This exercise is all sixteenth notes so again, only play as fast as you can play with control. And don't forget to use your metronome!

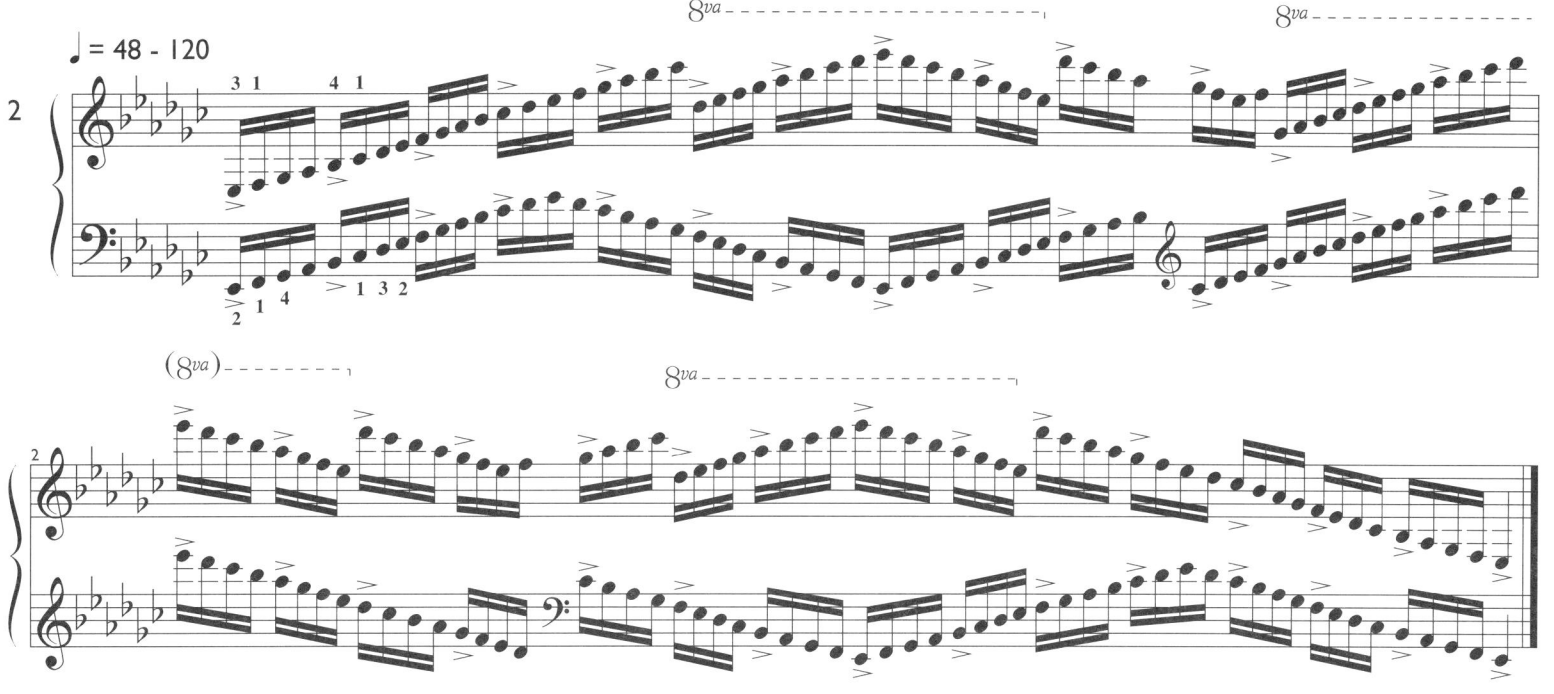

One more way to mix this up is to pick an interval. Let's use a 3rd. Use the same pattern as above, only with one hand starting on the root and one hand starting on the 3rd. The example below is in F♯ Harmonic Minor. Notice how the fingerings are consistent in relation to the root. While the left hand starts on finger 4, the right hand starts on finger 1 because that is the usual finger for A in the F♯ Minor scale (F♯=finger 2, G♯=finger 3, A=finger 1, etc.). You will find this much more challenging than the example above. You should also experiment with other intervals.

ARPEGGIOS

It's a good idea to choose one scale pattern and one arpeggio pattern for your daily warm-up, alternating the patterns each day. Arpeggio exercises are pretty much identical to scale exercises, except that (you guessed it) you play arpeggios instead of scales. The same rules apply. Use a metronome and choose a tempo that is both challenging and controllable. If you can master the following exercises, you can play in any progressive rock band.

> ### Note:
> If you feel any pain while doing these or any other exercises then STOP! Like any muscular development, it takes time to play through all these exercises in all keys at fast tempos. Start slowly and build endurance. If it hurts, stop for the day and try again tomorrow.

The following example utilizes an E Dominant 7th arpeggio. Do this in all the keys with all the 7th chords (major 7, min7♭5, minor 7) and triads. Do this over time, not all in one day!

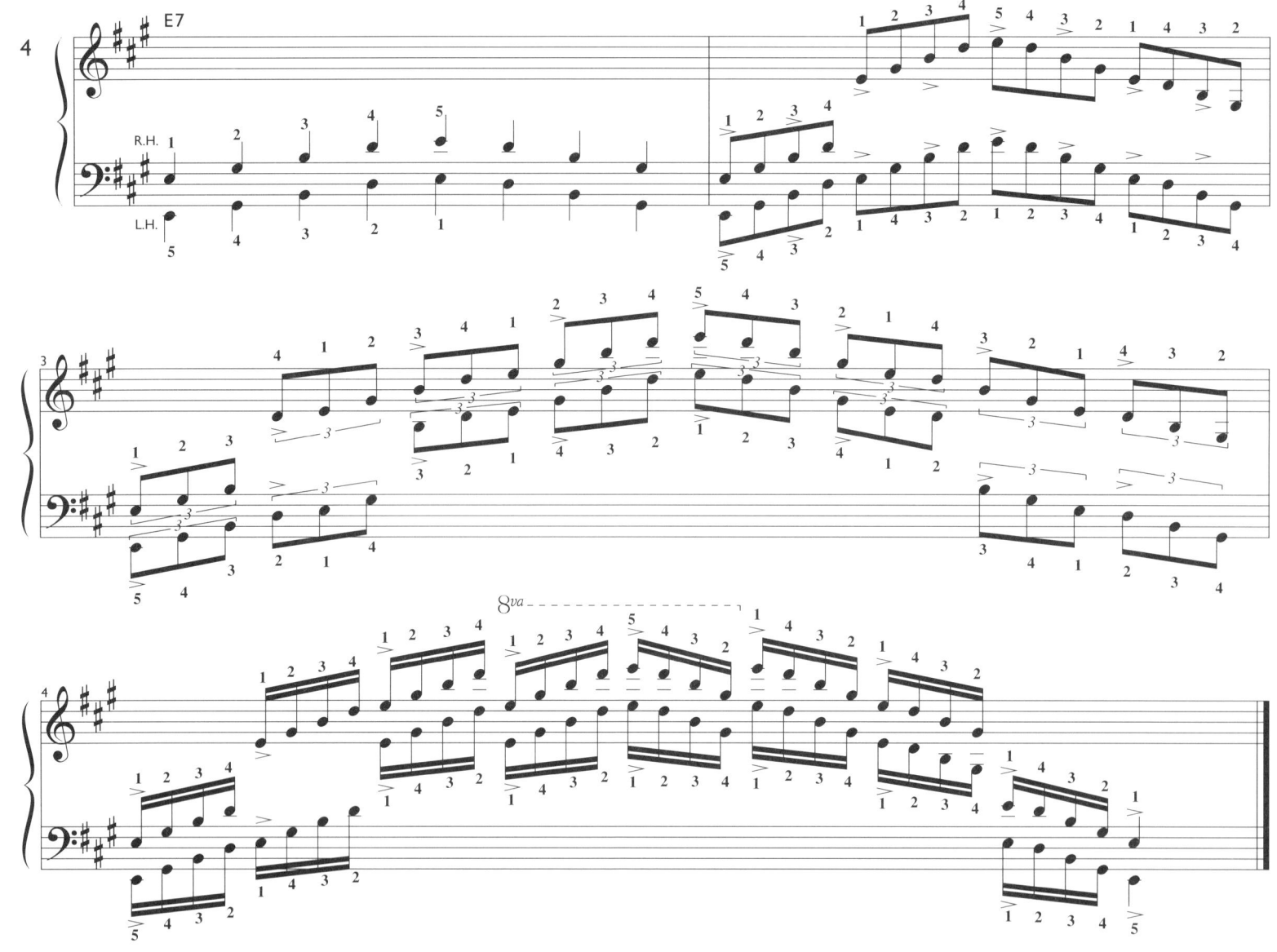

Here are some more arpeggio patterns. They are much like the scale patterns on page 21.

The following example utilizes a C Diminished arpeggio. Again, do this in all keys and, eventually, with all the chord types. Watch your fingerings and don't forget the metronome!

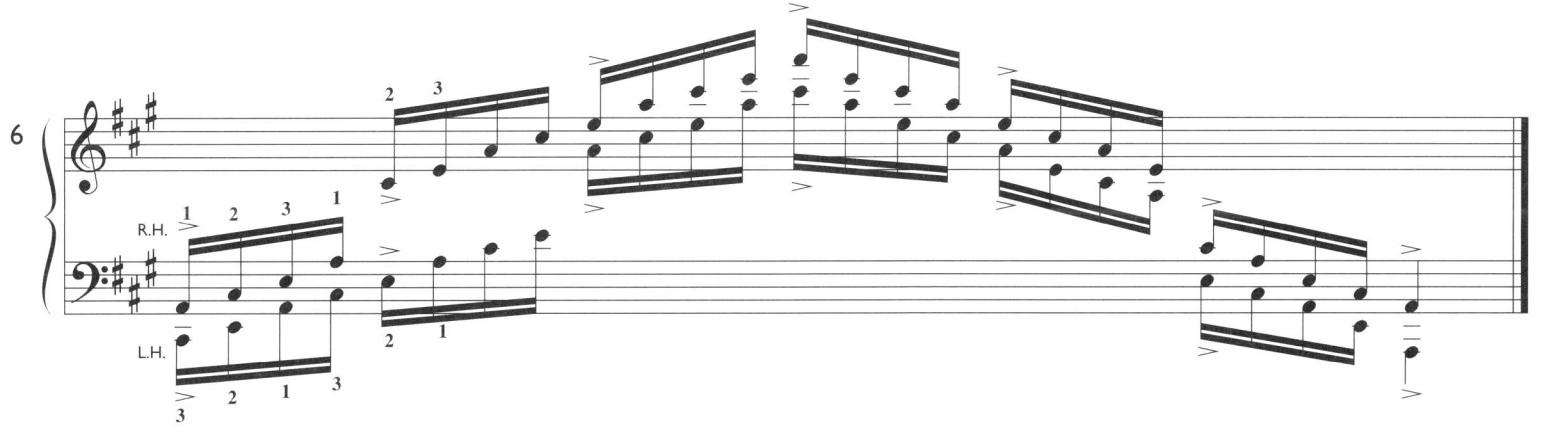

Here is a way to "mix up" your triad arpeggios, making them more interesting and challenging. Pick an interval, then ascend and descend four octaves in sixteenth notes.

The following uses the A Major triad arpeggio. Again, do this exercise in all major and minor keys.

ETUDES

The following pages are *etudes* (pieces that emphasize a specific technique) incorporating scales and arpeggios to get your left and right hands working together. They will help your technique and give you something other than straight scales and arpeggios to play. At this level, you should also be playing two- and three-part inventions by J. S. Bach, as well as other classical pieces. You may even want to pick up a book written specifically for developing technique. There are many on the market, such as the Hanon studies published by Alfred.

Try the following *Etude in E Minor*. Note that there are times when the left hand crosses over the right hand and then back again. This is a good way to get your left hand more "involved" with the piece and working independently of the right hand. This technique is very important. You may find yourself in an ensemble situation where the keyboard parts are not only more complex, but require you to play more than one keyboard at a time. This definitely requires the right and left hands to function completely independent of each other.

ETUDE IN E MINOR
Track 2

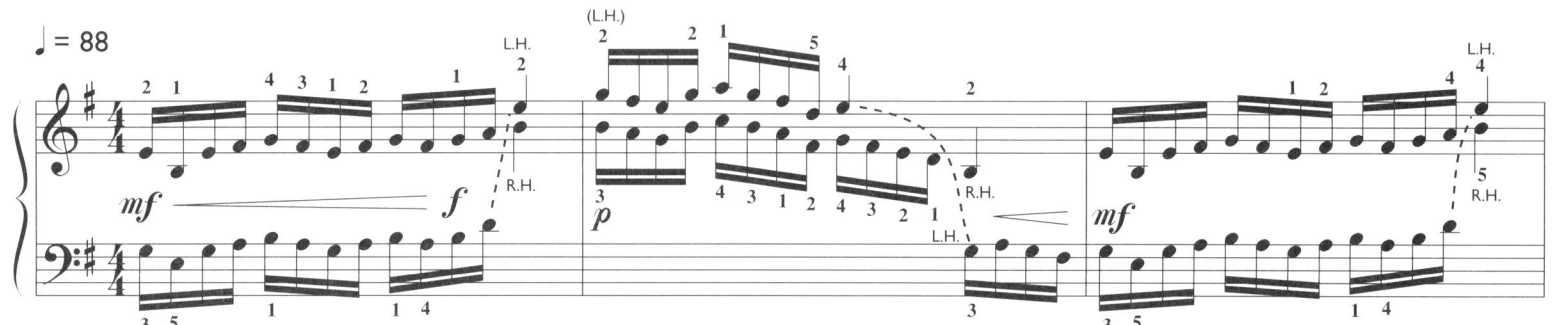

Here is an example in the style of a Bach two-part invention. You will see Bach's influence frequently in progressive rock music. Studying classical music will help you get your right and left hands to work not only together, but independently of each other.

BACH ROCKS
Track 3

CHAPTER 3

Accompanying vs. Part Playing vs. Soloing

ACCOMPANYING

When you are the accompanist, you are the sole "back-up" for a soloist. The soloist could be a singer or any other solo instrument (saxophone, trumpet, French horn, etc.). This means that *you* are the rhythm section. You must provide a groove (drummer), the foundation (bass player) and all the rhythm, harmonies, chords and fills (keyboard and guitar players). All this with your own two hands!

We call this *comping* (based on the word *accompany*) and it is actually not difficult (depending on the piece). Our goal can usually be attained by simply playing arpeggios or a walking bass in the left hand while playing chords and fills around the melody in the right hand.

Let's look at some typical accompaniment patterns.

8va---- = When 8va appears underneath, play that music one octave lower.

WALKING BASSLINE IN LEFT HAND WHILE COMPING CHORDS IN RIGHT HAND

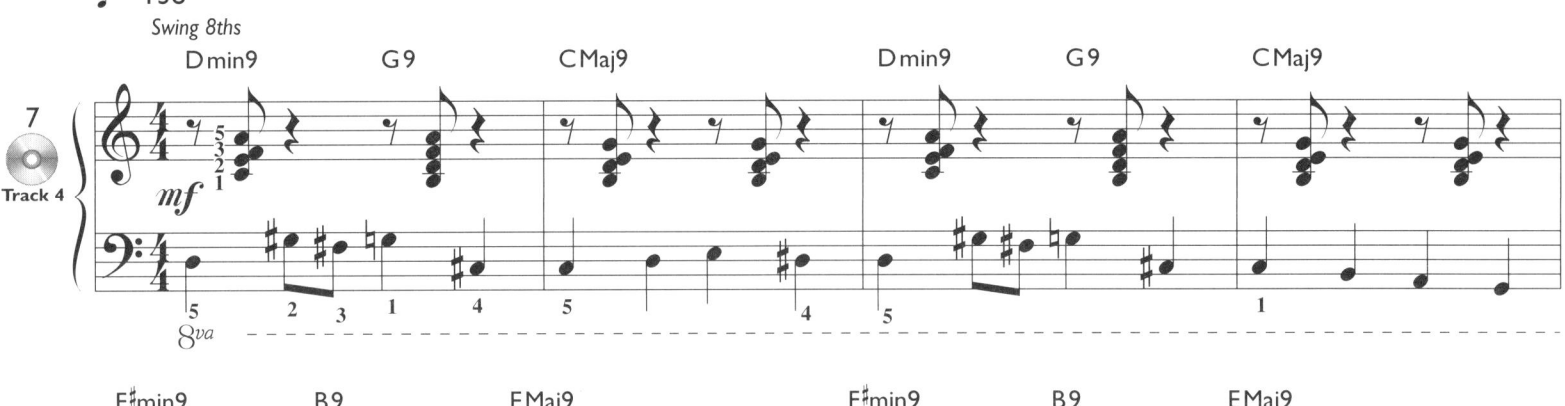

ARPEGGIATING AND PLAYING KEY NOTES IN AND AROUND THE MELODY

The melody notes are grey.

Obviously, if you are part playing, then you are "part" of something—part of a whole. This usually refers to an ensemble situation where the keyboard player plays a set part as opposed to improvised comping.

Here are a couple examples of possible keyboard parts in an ensemble situation. Note that some of the other instruments' parts are written out as well, so you can see how all of the parts fit together.

Always Coming Home is an example of a part to an instrumental rock ballad. It is played with the right hand and sounds best played on a synth with a bell/string combination sound.

 ALWAYS COMING HOME
Track 6

Ben Folds

*of the **Ben Folds Five***
is one of the hottest
young pianists
in contemporary music.
With their hit CD,
***Whatever and Ever Amen**,*
released in 1997,
they became well known
throughout the music world.
Ben is an accomplished player
capable of tender ballads in one song
and hard rocking pseudo-punk
in the next song.

This is an example of a possible mid-tempo rock piano part. The guitar part is shown above and the bass part is shown below. Notice the time signature ¢. This is *cut time*, which is also written $\frac{2}{2}$. The half note equals one beat.

WHY CAN'T WE?

Track 7

Soloing encompasses any situation where an instrument is featured. This could be anything from playing a solo piano piece to playing a featured part within an ensemble.

Following are some examples of possible solos. Hopefully, they will provide you with ideas to build on for your own solos.

This solo is a rock ballad for piano. It is not very technical, focusing mostly on the melodic material. A good solo doesn't need to be flashy!

ALL I NEED

This solo is more technically advanced, mainly featuring arpeggios in the right hand. Practice slowly at first and build up to the suggested tempo. Notice the *sextuplets*. Six notes are played in the time of four of the same value (in this case, six sixteenth notes in the time of four—one beat).

Track 9

IN SEARCH OF THE BROKEN CHORD

This solo is fairly technically advanced, but demonstrates that a flashy solo can be melodic, too.
Pay attention to the accent marks and the melodic content will be clearer.

TECHNICALLY TUNEFUL

Track 10

Serendipity is a progressive rock keyboard solo. Play it with a mini-Moog sound. Be expressive. Don't just read the notes. Practice slowly at first. This one will take a while to perfect. It's unlikely that a keyboard player would ever have to accommpany a solo like this with their left hand, so only a right-hand part is shown.

= Super triplet. Three notes in the time of a half note.

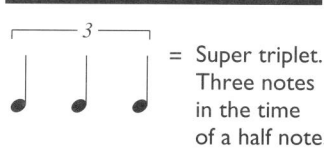

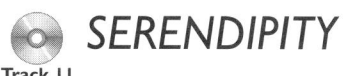

SERENDIPITY

Track 11

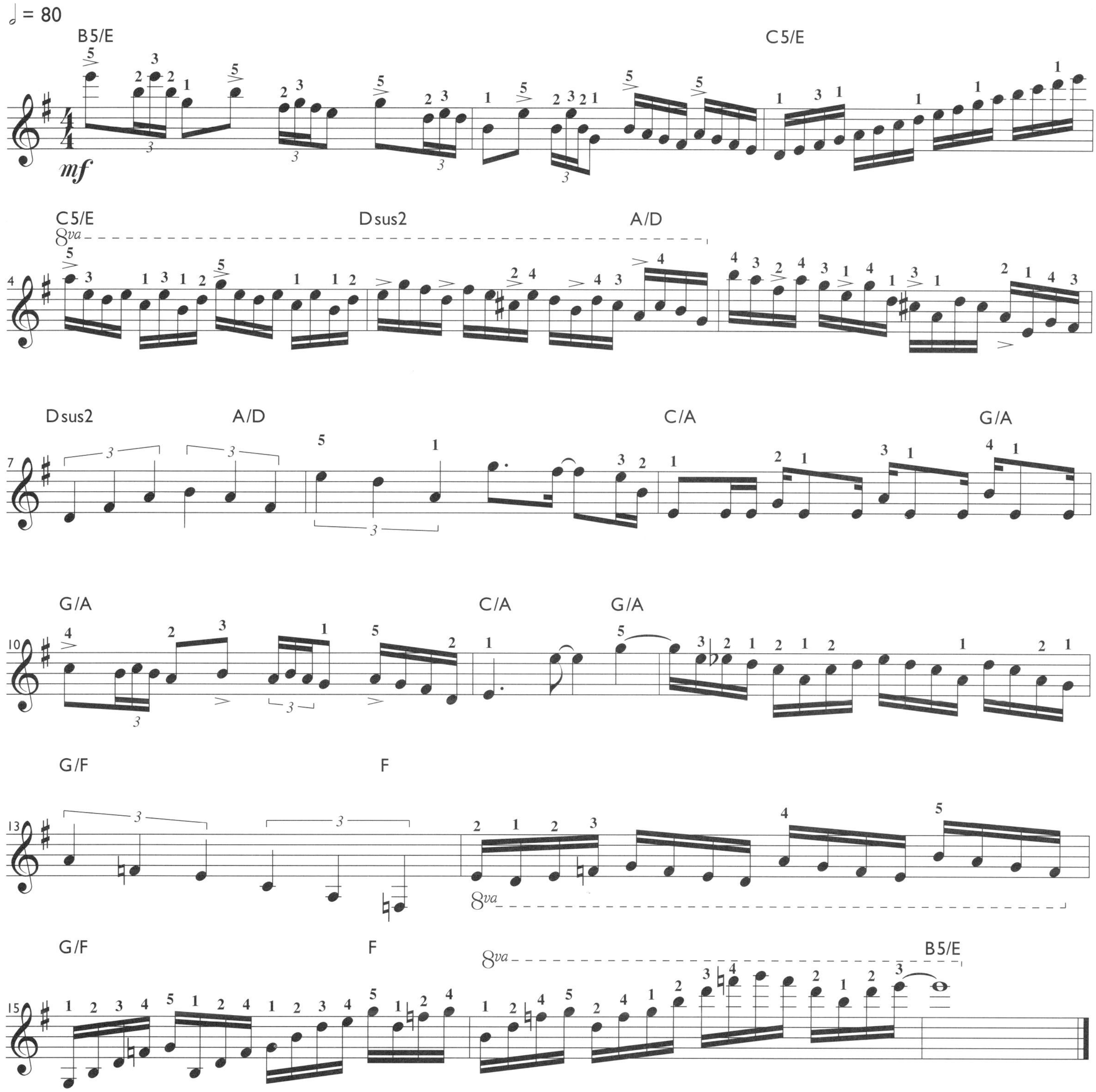

Exercise:

Hopefully, these pieces have gotten your creative juices flowing. Try to compose a solo of your own in each style demonstrated in this chapter.

CHAPTER 4

Harmony

EXTENSIONS

Let's look at some ways to make your music more interesting. A very common way to add interest and richness to your writing and playing is by use of *extensions*. Exensions are notes that are beyond the 7th, such as 9ths, 11ths and 13ths, or tones that are not diatonic at all, such as ♭9, ♯9, ♯11 and ♭13. Some theory books say that any note a whole step above a chord tone is an available extension. However, anything goes and ultimately, you should just use your ears to achieve the sound you desire.

First, let's explore the numeric names of the extensions. If you are a graduate of *Intermediate Rock Keyboards*, you know that the numbers are derived from an expanded major scale built on the root of the chord. In other words, if the chord in question has C as the root, the expanded major scale from which we derive the extension names is the C Major scale (see page 18).

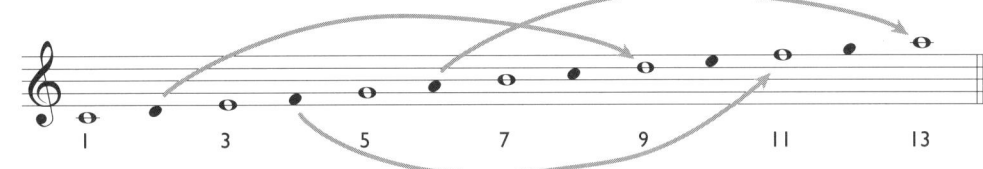

Below are examples of possible extensions available on various 6th and 7th chords. Try each one individually and experiment with their sounds.

Major 6th

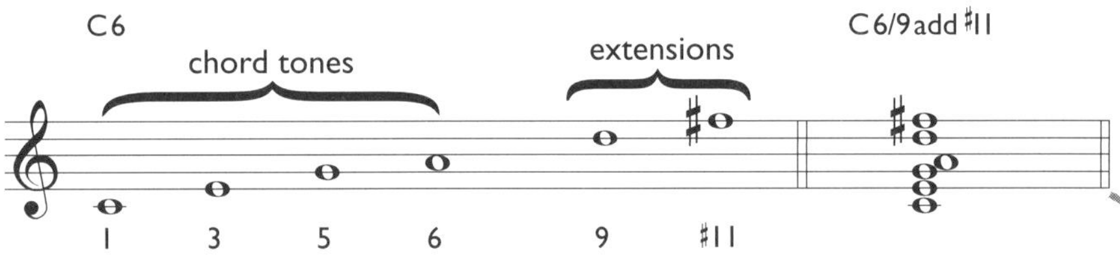

C6 — chord tones — extensions — C6/9 add ♯11
1 3 5 6 9 ♯11

A major 6th chord may include a major 7th or vice-versa.

Major 7th

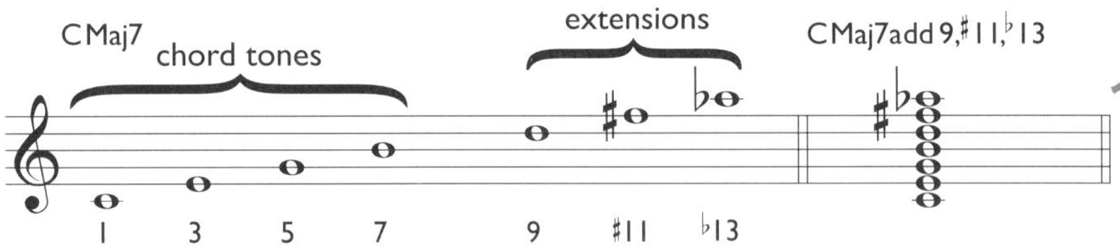

CMaj7 — chord tones — extensions — CMaj7 add 9, ♯11, ♭13
1 3 5 7 9 ♯11 ♭13

Minor 6th

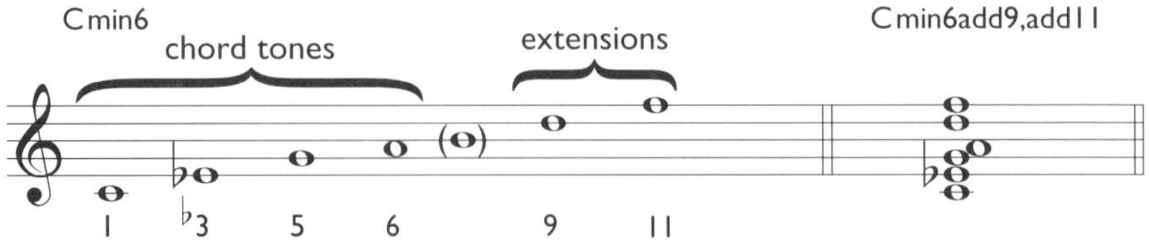

Cmin6 — chord tones — extensions — Cmin6 add9, add11
1 ♭3 5 6 9 11

A minor 6th chord may include a major 7th.

Minor 7th

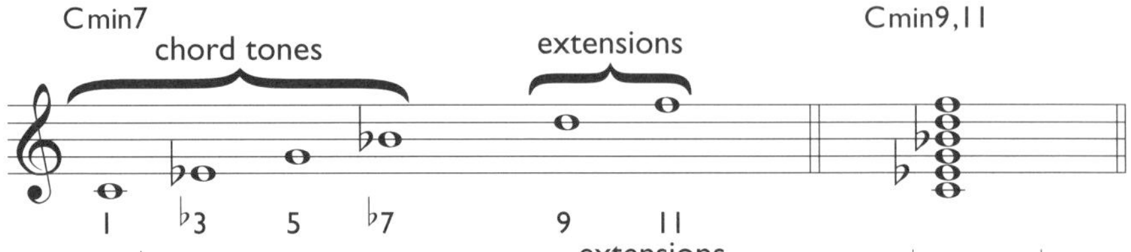

Cmin7 — chord tones — extensions — Cmin9,11
1 ♭3 5 ♭7 9 11

The 9 is not usually available on iii minor 7 chords.

Minor 7th ♭5

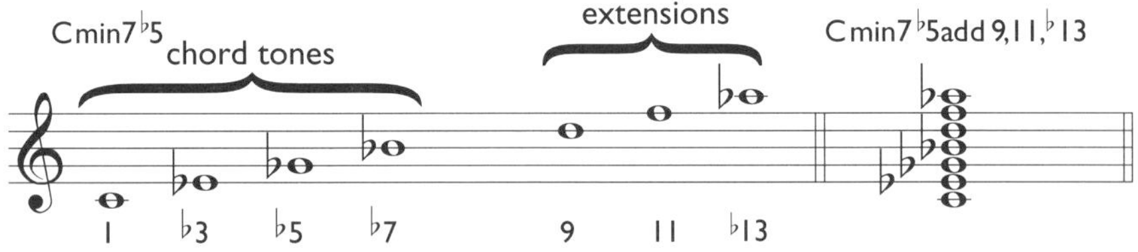

Cmin7♭5 — chord tones — extensions — Cmin7♭5 add 9,11,♭13
1 ♭3 ♭5 ♭7 9 11 ♭13

The 9 is not usually available unless it is diatonic to the key.

Dominant 7th Suspended 4th

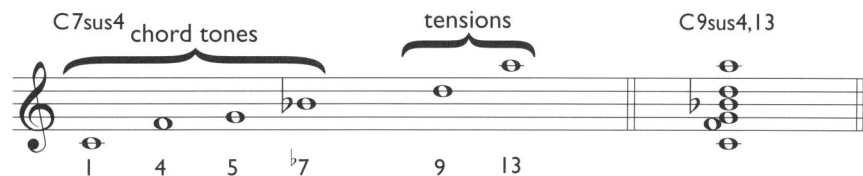

Augmented 7th

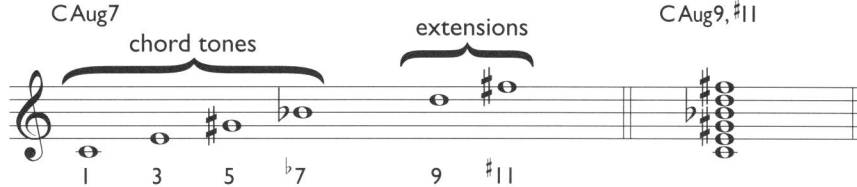

Diminished 7th

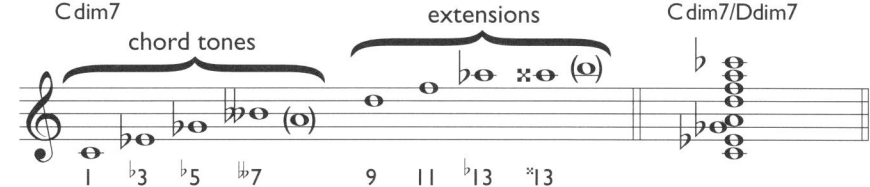

The °13 only occurs over dim7 chords. Notice that some notes can be respelled enharmonically for easier reading.

Dominant 7th

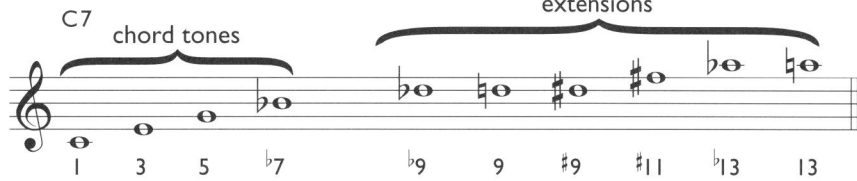

𝄪 = Double sharp. Raise the note a whole step.
♭♭ = Double flat. Lower the note a whole step.

In the major 7th and dominant 7th chords, you will notice the use of extensions that are technically "not available," because they are not diatonic. The use of the extensions ♭9, ♯9, ♯11, or ♭13 alters the quality of the chord. Therefore, a dominant 7 or major 7 containing one or more of these altered extensions becomes an *altered chord*. Note that ♭9 and ♯9 are not considered usable extensions for the altered major 7 chord.

COMBINING EXTENSIONS

There are several possible extension combinations for the dominant 7th chord:

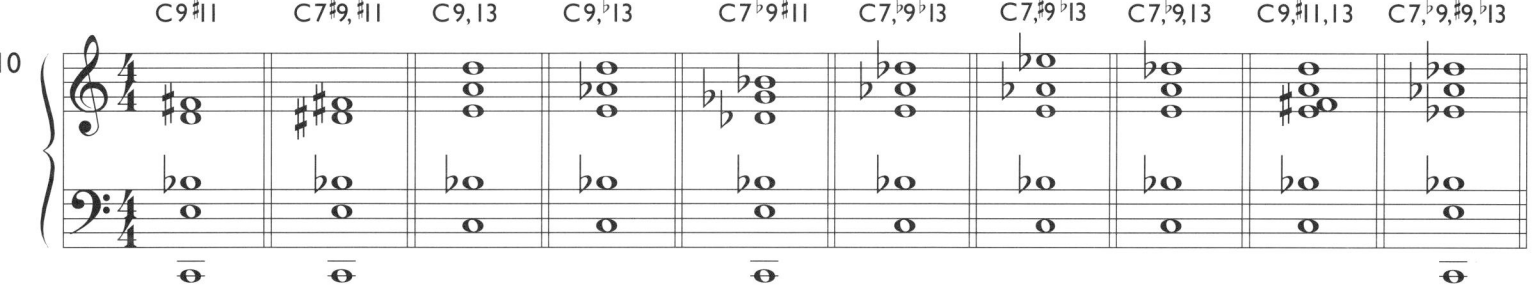

You will notice the use of extensions in chapters to come. Try to get used to them and learn to recognize their sounds. As the style of rock'n'roll progressed, it drew more and more schooled and refined musicians. They brought the style to new heights by using some of the harmonic, compositional and arranging techniques we will touch on in this chapter and the next.

EXTENSIONS IN CHORD PROGRESSIONS

Now let's take a look at a couple of chord progressions, and compare the way they sound with and without extensions. Play the blocked chords. The point of this exercise is to hear the depth and richness the extensions add. Hopefully, you will hear the difference right away.

11

Track 12

Here is a chord progression in D with no extensions:

The same chord progression in D with extensions:

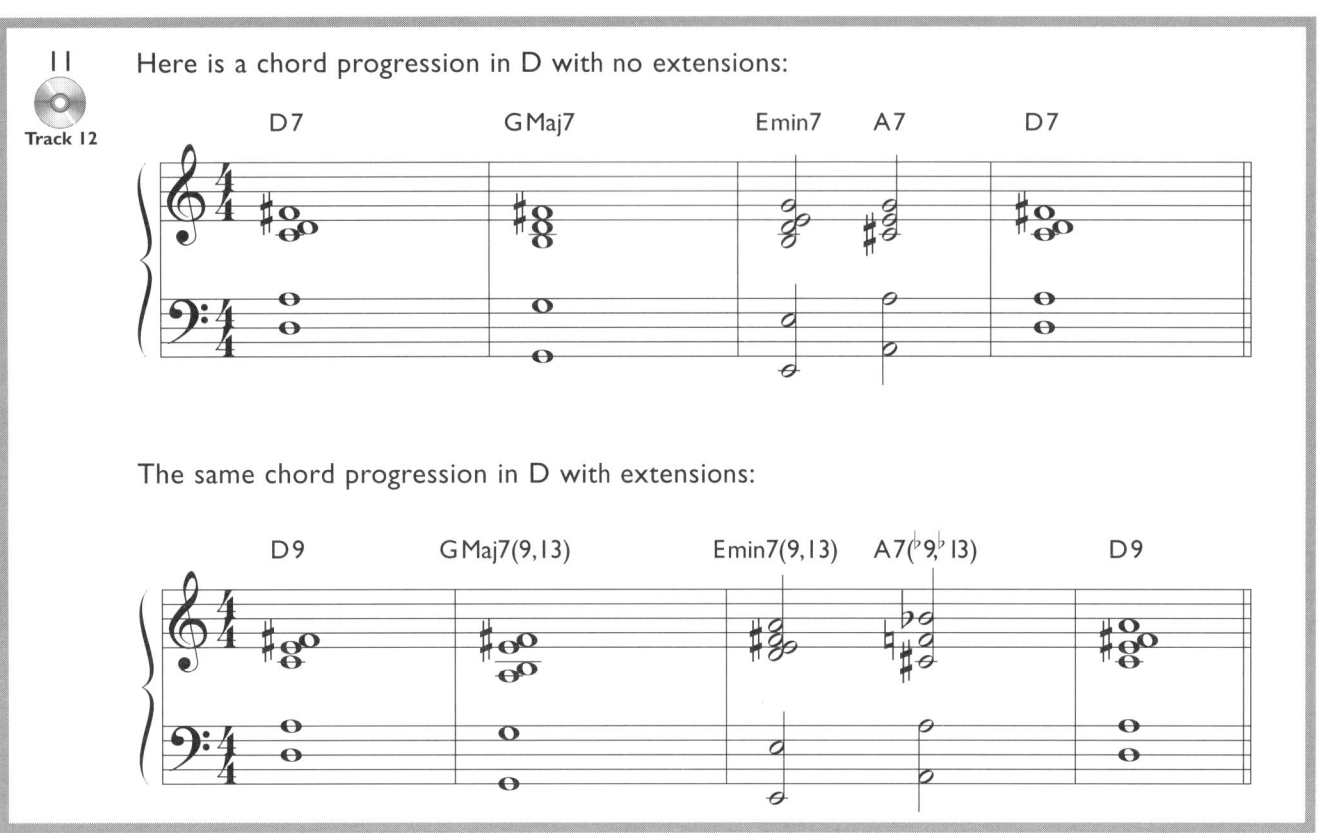

12

Track 13

Here is a chord progression in B Minor with no extensions:

The same chord progression in B Minor with extensions:

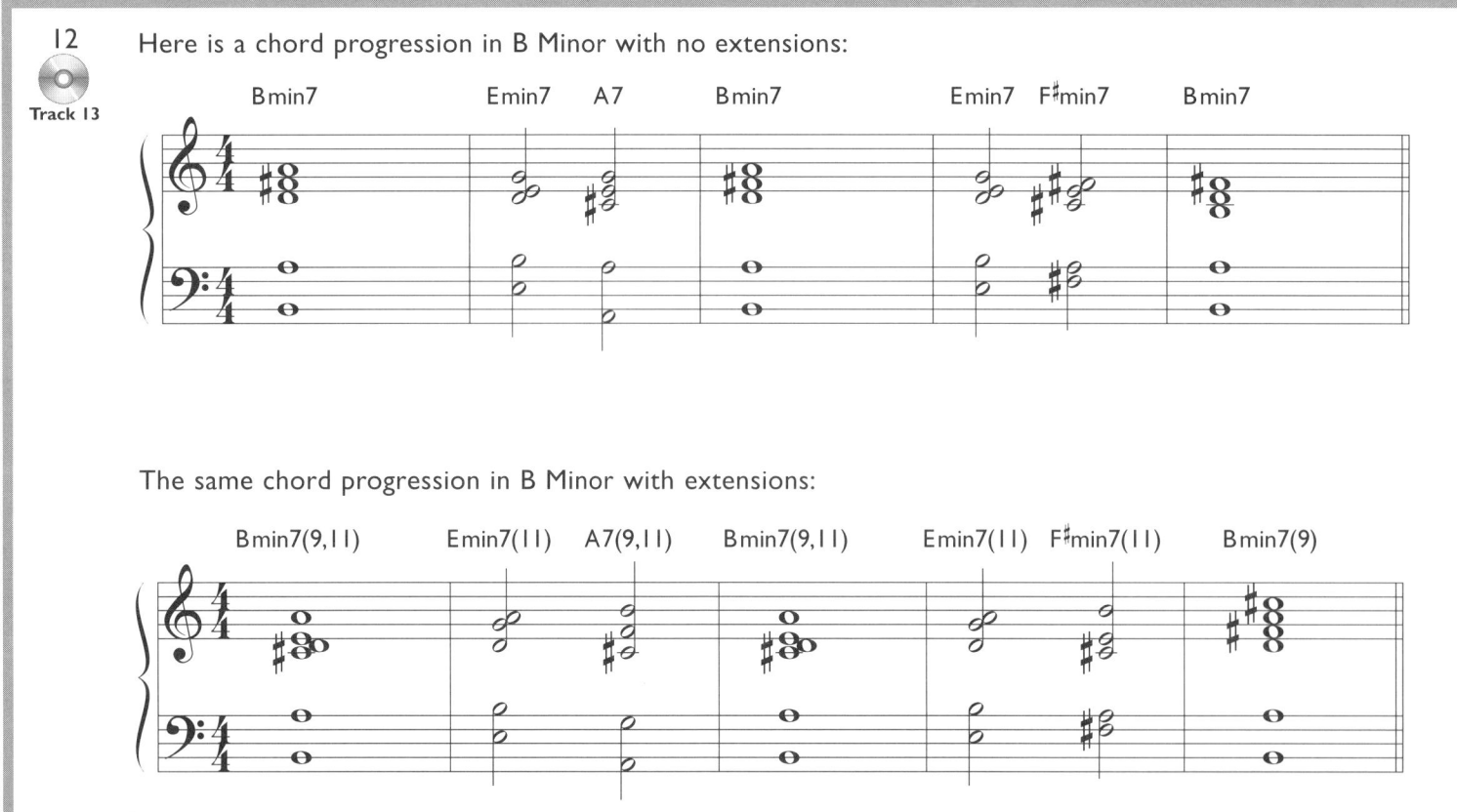

CHAPTER 5

Soloing

There are three main tools for rock improvisation:

Modes
Scales
Arpeggios

Each tool involves a different thought process and results in a different sound. Let's investigate each approach.

MODES

The modes of the major scale were introduced in *Beginning Rock Keyboard* and *Intermediate Rock Keyboard*. They are also reviewed on page 19 of this book. As a reminder, below is a C Major scale showing the name of the mode that is built on each scale degree.

Playing the C Major scale, starting and ending on the indicated scale degree, will result in the indicated mode. For example, playing the C Major scale from the 2nd degree (D above middle C to the D an octave above), creates the D Dorian mode. Each mode has its own individual sound. Learn to identify them by ear and get comfortable with how they feel on the keyboard. Example 13 is a quick review of which mode begins on each step of the major scale.

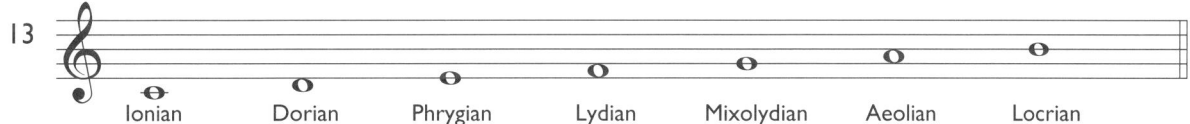

RELATING DIATONIC HARMONIZATION TO THE MODES

Diatonic harmonization of the major scale is based on *tertiary* (ter-shi-ar-ē: characterized by or based on the number three) harmony. The various degrees of the scale are harmonized in 3rds, thus creating triads and 7th chords. Since the modes of the major scale are all strictly diatonic—that is, they are merely a re-ordering of the major scale—the harmonies derived from the scale can be modal, as well.

Here is a quick review, showing the C Major scale and its diatonic 7th chords. We can call this the *C Major chord scale*.

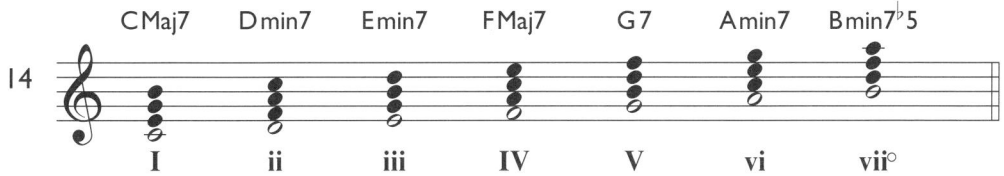

Each chord in the major chord scale (page 37) can be thought of as characterizing a particular mode of the scale. For example, if we want to improvise over a min7 chord, our choices are narrowed down to three possible modes, Dorian, Phrygian and Aeolian, because they are the only three modes that contain the notes of a min7 chord (1, ♭3, 5, ♭7). You can use any one of these three modes to solo over a min7 chord.

Now, if we play a *vamp* (a short progression that repeats over and over), such as Dmin7 to G7, our possibilities narrow to just one modal chord scale: D Dorian. D Dorian is the only mode of the major scale whose chord scale accommodates a minor 7th chord on i and a dominant 7th built on IV. To see this easily, take the major chord scale on page 37 and re-order it so that Dmin7 is i. This is the D Dorian chord scale.

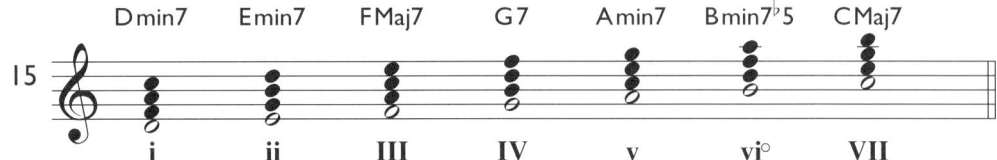

We can use this easy method to create many wonderful little chord vamps for practicing modal improvisation. If you have a sequencer, or any means of home recording, set up the following vamps over which to practice soloing. If you don't have the means to do this, then just try playing the chords with your left hand while soloing with your right hand. Better yet, find someone to jam with. If you have the CD that is available for this book, jam along with the band!

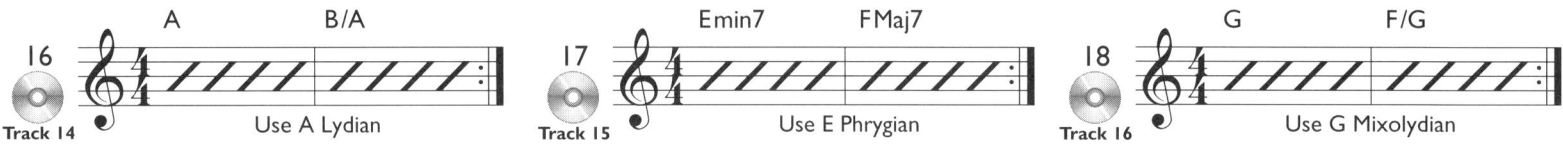

ARPEGGIOS

As you learned in *Beginning Rock Keyboard*, an arpeggio is the notes of a chord played separately, one at a time. You can use your knowledge of the chord scales to make arpeggios a tool for improvisation. For example, for our D Dorian vamp (Dmin7 to G7), we have the harmonized chords of the D Dorian chord scale available to arpeggiate. Look at the D Dorian chord scale shown above and try arpeggiating each harmony a few different ways. Now, try playing any and all of these arpeggios over the Dorian vamp. Have fun!

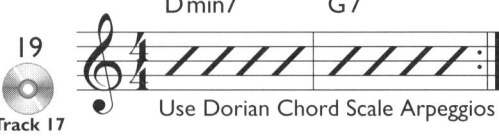

PENTATONIC SCALES

By now, you are well acquainted with both the major and minor pentatonic scales. You know they are five-note scales, derived from the major scale, with these formulas:

Major = 1, 2, 3, 5, 6   **Minor = 1, ♭3, 4, 5, ♭7**

You also know that they relate to each other in much the same way that the major scales relate to their relative minor—C Major pentatonic and A Minor pentatonic have the same notes but in a different order, one starting on C and the other on A.

The major pentatonic scale can be used over any major triad or major 7th chord. The minor pentatonic scale is used over any minor triad or minor 7th chord. Of course, there is always someone ready to throw all caution to the wind and use minor pentatonic scales over major triads and 7th chords, especially in a blues context.

Here is a standard minor twelve-bar blues in G, using a dominant chord on V. Try several approaches to improvising over this:

1. Play only the G Minor Pentatonic scale throughout.
2. Switch to D Major Pentatonic to play over the V chord, D7.
3. Play the minor pentatonic scale built on the root of each chord: G Minor Pentatonic on Gmin7 chords, C Minor Pentatonic on the Cmin7 chord and D Minor and/or D Major Pentatonic on the D7.

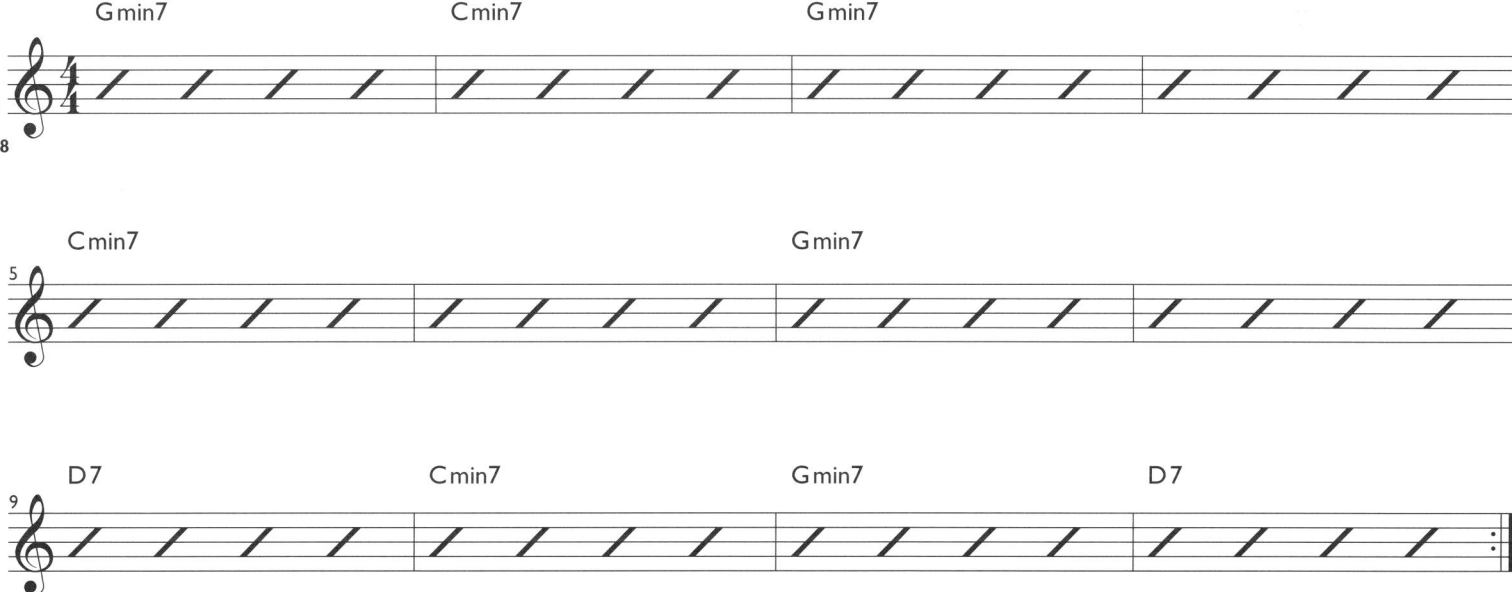

INFLECTIONS

Put a personal stamp on your playing! Use dynamics when you play, along with your pitch bend and modulation wheels for bending, sliding and vibrato. These techniques, a good ear and sense of rhythm separate the great players from the rest.

DIATONIC HARMONIZATION OF THE MELODIC AND HARMONIC MINOR SCALES

On page 37, we harmonized a C Major scale and talked about it's relation to modal harmony. Now let's delve into some more advanced theory and look at the melodic and harmonic minor scales.

MELODIC MINOR

First, let's harmonize the melodic minor scale. Below is a C Melodic Minor chord scale.

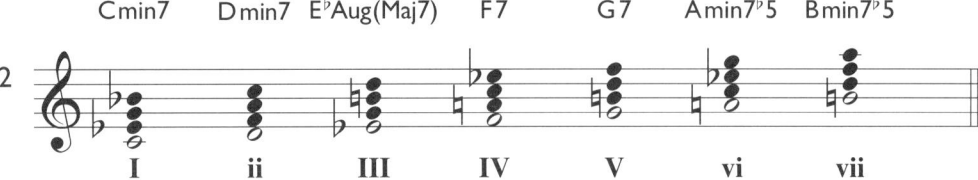

Note: *In classical theory, we think of the melodic minor as descending differently than it ascends. It ascends as shown here, and descends in the natural minor. In rock and jazz, we think of it only in the ascending form. This is sometimes called jazz minor, but is just as often called melodic minor, even though it does not descend in the traditional way.*

Now, let's take a look at the modes that occur on each degree of the melodic minor scale. These modes are slight variations of the major scale modes. For example, the 2nd mode of the melodic minor scale is just like the Dorian mode of the major scale, except that when compared to the Dorian mode, it has a ♭2. That is why we call it the *Dorian* ♭2.

HARMONIC MINOR

Now let's look at the harmonic minor chord scale. Below is a C Harmonic Minor chord scale.

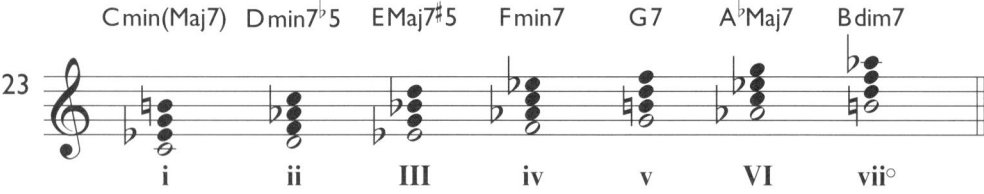

Now let's look at the modes derived from the harmonic minor scale. Here are the modes of the C Harmonic Minor scale.

Practical application of this information only becomes fluid with a lot of practice. The best way to learn where, when and how to use the correct scales is to analyze other peoples' solos. You should also play along with recorded solos and compose your own (on paper). Also, you must learn to recognize each individual mode when you hear it. Playing modes as your scale warm-up exercises will help you do this. Your goal is to become spontaneously inventive with this material.

For your reference, below is a chart showing various chord types and the scales or modes that are appropriate to use when improvising over them.

CHORD AND SCALE USE CHART

Chord Type	Mode or Scale		Chord Type	Mode or Scale
Maj7	Ionian		Unaltered	Mixolydian
	Lydian		Dominant 7	Lydian ♭7
	Lydian #2			Mixolydian #6
	Major Pentatonic			Phrygian Dominant

Chord Type	Mode or Scale		Chord Type	Mode or Scale
Min 7	Dorian		Min7(♭5)	Locrian
	Phrygian			Aeolian ♭5
	Dorian ♭2			Locrian #6
	Lydian ♭3 ♭7			Super Locrian*
	Minor Pentatonic			*(usually used in an altered dominant situation)

Chord Type	Mode or Scale		Chord Type	Mode or Scale
Min(Maj7)	Melodic Minor		Maj7(#5)	Lydian #5
	Harmonic Minor			Ionian #5

Chord Type	Mode or Scale
Dim7	7th Mode Harmonic Minor

MODAL INTERCHANGE AND PARALLEL MODES

Another way to add interest to your music is by introducing non-diatonic notes or chords. In the key of C, for example, you may want to use an A♭ chord. This can be done through *modal interchange*. Modal interchange involves "borrowing" chords from different modes of the same scale-type. We usually don't borrow chords from modes made from other types of scales. If we are in a major key, for instance, we don't usually borrow chords from the modes of the harmonic minor scale. Here's an example: the Aeolian mode is a mode of the major scale. When playing in C Major, if we sneak in a chord from C Aeolian—using another mode of the major scale but keeping the C root—we are applying the principal of *modal interchange*. The chord from C Aeolian, such as A♭, is a *borrowed chord*. We can use C Dorian, C Phrygian, C Lydian, etc. in the same manner. The borrowed chord suggests the sound of its own mode without actually switching to that mode. In theory, any chord from any mode of the scale of the piece is a potential modal interchange or borrowed chord. Some are used more frequently than others, while some almost never occur.

Two of the most common progressions found in rock'n'roll include modal interchange chords.

> **I, ♭VII, ♭VI, ♭VII**   This progression is EVERYWHERE in rock'n'roll.

First we have the major I chord, which is diatonic to any major mode. Second is the ♭VII major chord, which gives us a sense that this is a Mixolydian progression, because the Mixolydian mode has the ♭7 degree and the chord built on it is major. Grab a piece of music paper and write out a Mixolydian chord scale—it's a good exercise and you will demonstrate this point for yourself.

But then... the ♭VI major chord. OH NO! This chord does not exist in the Mixolydian mode or any other major mode for that matter! What could it be? It must be a modal interchange chord. There are two modes of the major scale that have a ♭VI major chord: the Aeolian and Phrygian modes. Prove it. Write out the chord scales for those modes.

Play the chords below and hear how this sounds. It will probably sound quite natural since, whether you realize it or not, you've heard this many, many times in rock music.

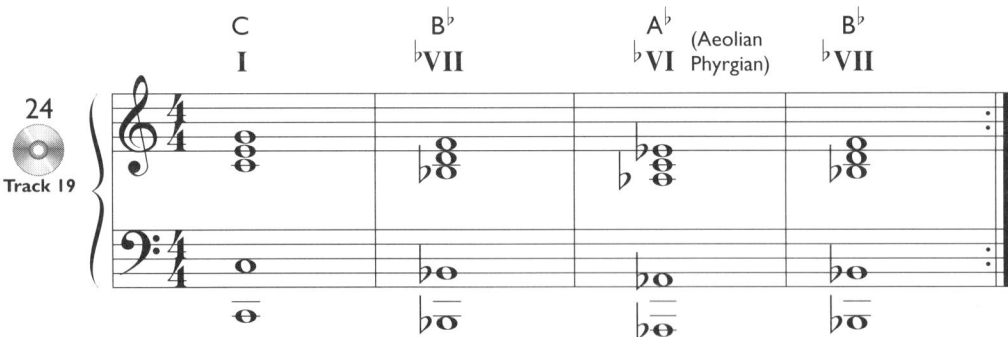

Here's a typical major progression with a borrowed ♭VI major chord. Once again, we are borrowing from the Aeolian or Phrygian mode. This progression was used a lot by Yes, Genesis and even Nirvana.

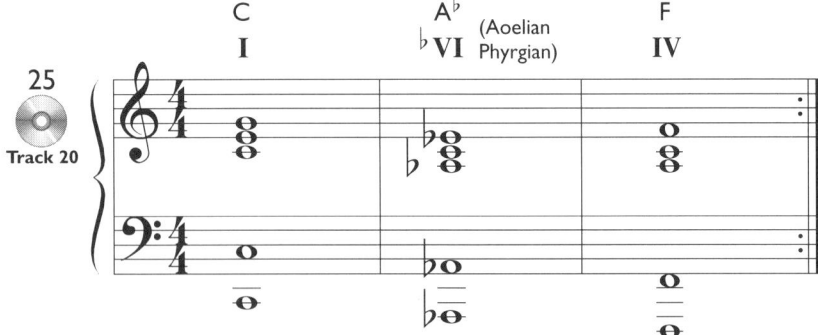

MODAL INTERCHANGE CADENCES

Let's look at some *cadences* that utilize modal interchange. A cadence is the resolution of a progression. It encompasses the chords that end the progression. The first example below is a very basic, diatonic chord progression: I major, IV major, V major and back to I major. The last two chords are the cadence because the V major chord resolves back to I major. V major to I major is a very commonly used cadence.

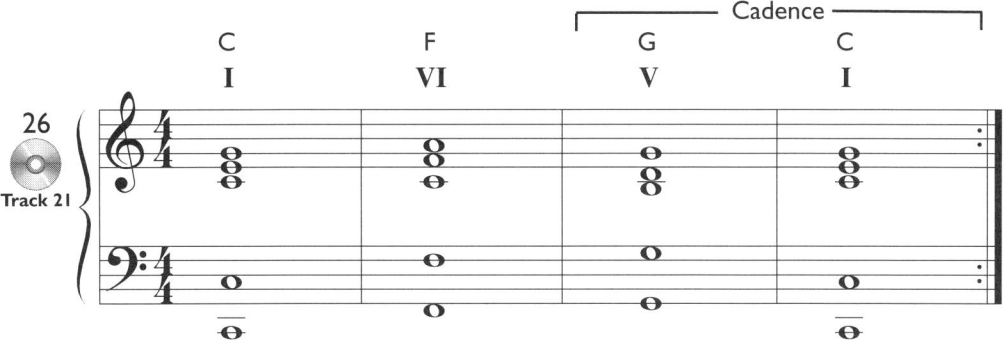

Now let's substitute a modal interchange or borrowed chord for the V chord. We'll hear the same progression as before but with a different cadence. In the example below, the ♭VII major chord from Mixolydian is substituted for the V major chord. This makes a ♭VII major to I major cadence, which is also a very common cadence.

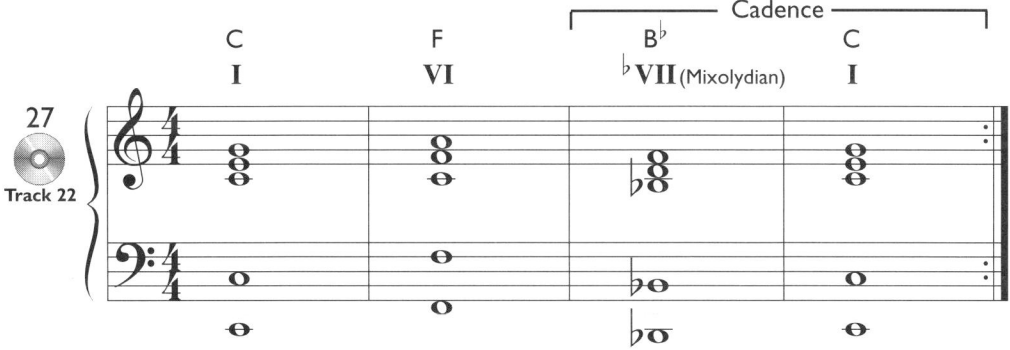

Other commonly used cadences utilizing modal interchange chords:

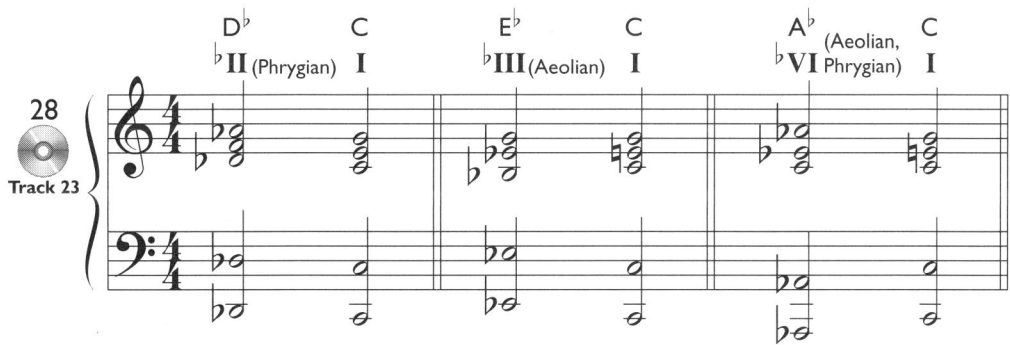

Here's a tune for you to play. This is in the key of D Minor, so it is essentially a D Aeolian (natural minor) progression. The concept of modal interchange works with a minor key, too. Thinking of it as being in D Aeolian leaves you with all of your good old, familiar modes of the major scale for use in modal interchange.

Try to find the modal interchange chords. If you found the E♭ Major chord in bars 3 and 7, and the D Major chord in bars 8 and 9, then you are correct. The E♭ Major chord (♭II major) is being borrowed from the parallel Phrygian mode (D Phrygian), and the D Major chord is being borrowed from the parallel Ionian mode (D Major).

SOMEDAY

Track 24

The Form:

Play up to the repeat in the 1st ending. Then, repeat the first three measures and skip the first ending, playing the second ending instead. Play the next four-bar section twice, then go back to the beginning. Play the whole piece with no repeats (skipping the first ending) and end with the last measure (*Fine*).

Now try your hand at a solo. *Moon Beams* is a progressive rock keyboard solo, which sounds great played with a mini moog sound. The scales or modes being used are indicated in parentheses. This is a D Aeolian progression, but there are also some modal interchange chords. The E7 chord in bars 25 through 28 is borrowed from the parallel Lydian mode (D Lydian) so the note choices are from the A Major scale, the relative major scale to D Lydian. Also, the F#7,11 chord in bars 13 through 20 is functioning as the V of the B Minor chord, to which it resolves. This is called a *secondary dominant* (any dominant chord that resolves up a 4th but is not part of the key) and it adds a little tension and dissonance to the progression.

CHAPTER 6

Building Intensity

In this chapter, we will explore techniques for adding interest and building intensity in your songs. The first of these is the use of *pedal tones*.

PEDAL TONES

A pedal tone is a single bass note sustained through a series of chord changes. It derives its name from the organ, whose pedals are arranged like a keyboard for bass notes. The pedal tone is usually sustained on the tonic (I) or dominant (V) note of the key. The chord analysis is usually indicated with slash chords, where the chord name is to the left of the slash, and the bass note is to the right. For example, F/E♭ denotes an F chord with an E♭ in the bass.

Below are some examples of common chord progressions using pedal tones. Try playing them to get familiar with how this technique sounds. You will hear the strong feeling of continuity it creates within the key, thus making a high level of tension and dissonance acceptable. In other words, even "wrong" notes sound good as long as they resolve to consonant notes.

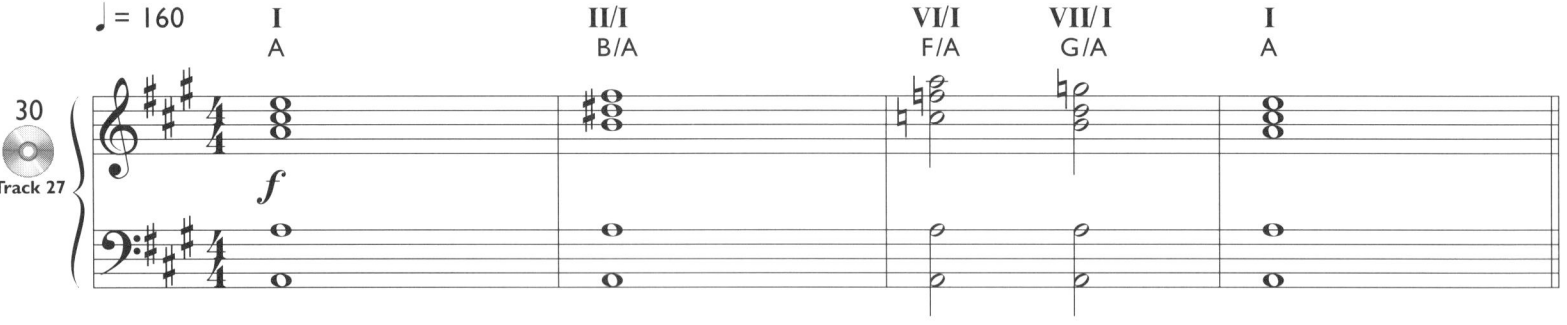

Compare the following two examples to hear the difference pedal tones can make. The right-hand part is the same in both examples, but the left-hand parts (bass notes) are different. The bass notes in Example 32 change with each chord, sustaining the roots of the chords, while the bass notes in Example 33 are pedal tones.

Tony Banks *was one of the original members of Genesis. Founded in 1967, more as a songwriters' collective than a virtuoso group, it also included Peter Gabriel and, eventually, Phil Collins.*

This tune makes extensive use of pedal tones. Have fun!

PUT THE PEDAL TO THE METAL

Track 31

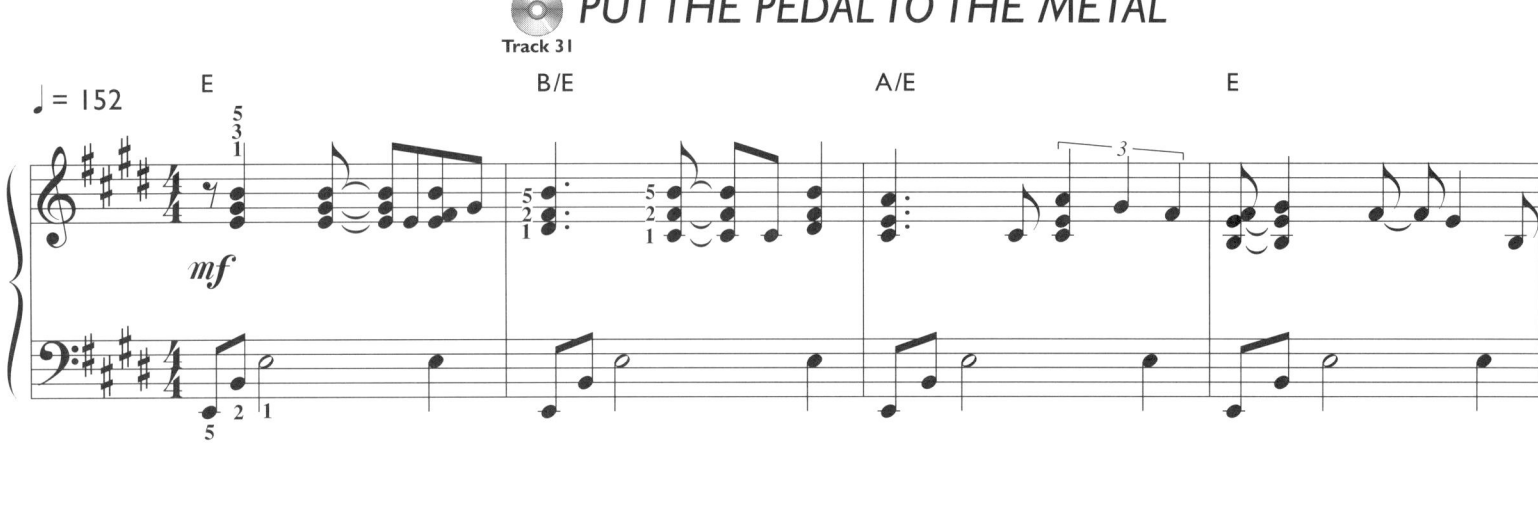

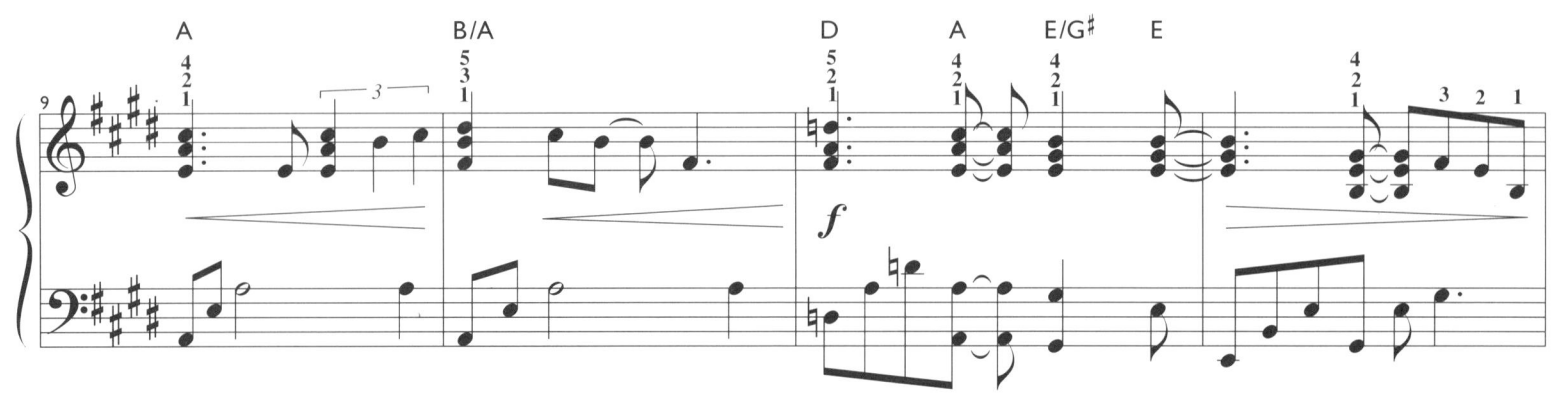

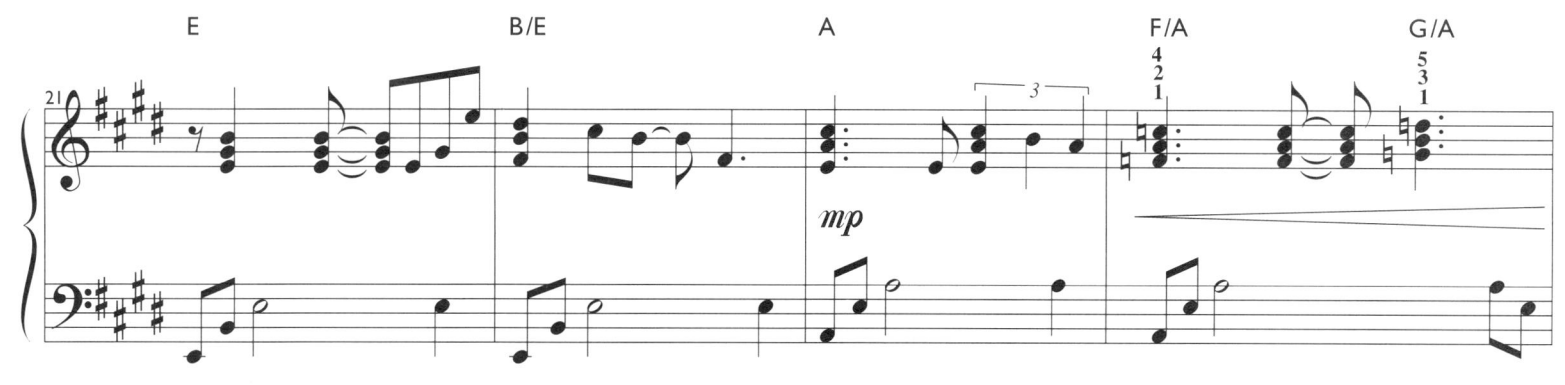

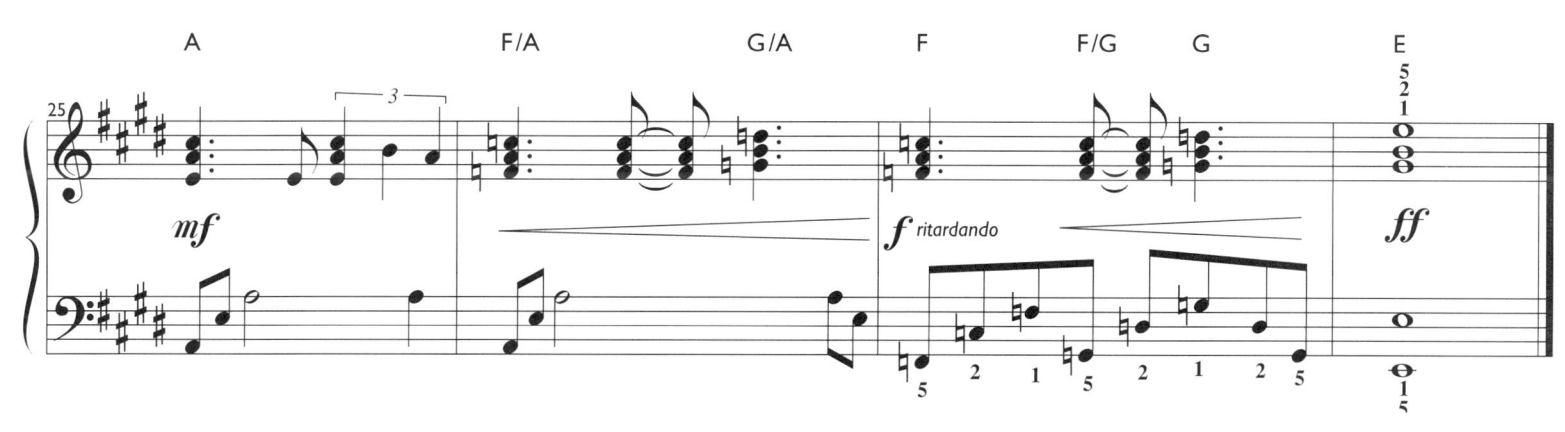

OSTINATO

An *ostinato* is an accompaniment figure, or phrase, that is repeated. Where a pedal tone establishes a single bass tone beneath a series of chord changes, an ostinato involves multiple notes. Like a pedal tone, ostinatos usually occur as a bass figure. They usually emphasize the tonic of a key and are often used to convey strong rhythmic ideas.

Because they establish such a strong sense of tonality, pedal tones and ostinato are very effective in modal contexts. An ostinato can include the tonic, and other characteristic notes, of a mode.

Let's look at some commonly used ostinato figures.

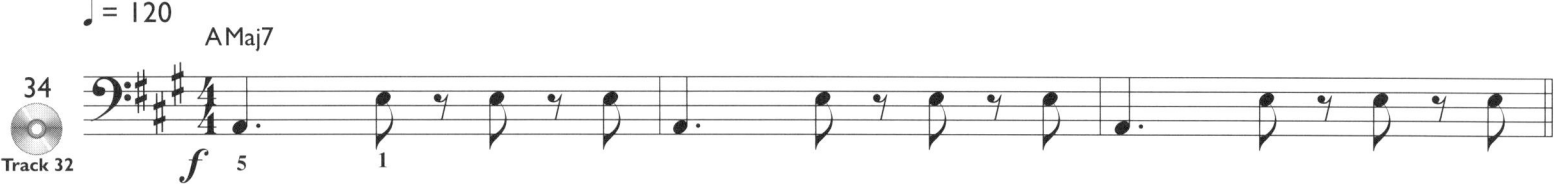

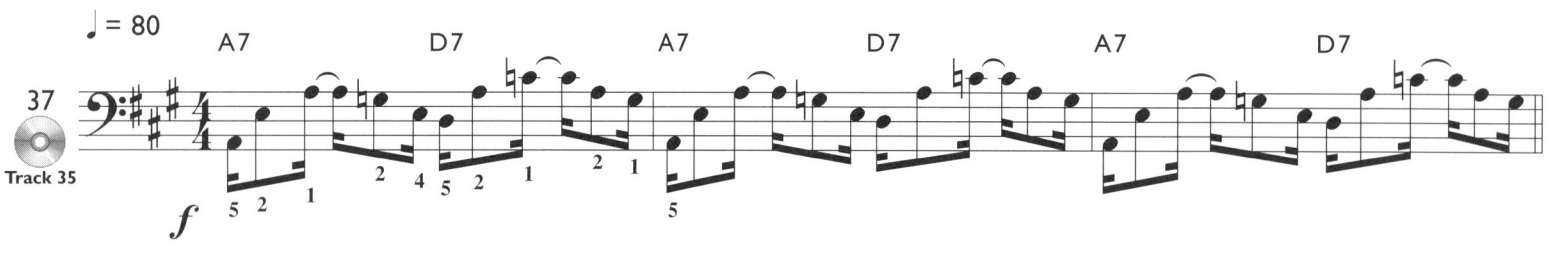

The following tune emphasizes the use of ostinato in the left hand, while comping rhythms are used in the right hand. Focus on the groove with the left hand. Otherwise, the part becomes just a bunch of repeating notes. The key is to establish a strong foundation and groove. The rhythm part in the right hand should augment and substantiate what the left hand is playing.

OSTINATO GROOVE
Track 36

MODULATION

Modulation is the melodic and/or harmonic movement from one key into another. In order for a modulation to occur, the original *tonal center* (in the key of C Major, C is the tonal center) must be shifted to a new one.

DIRECT MODULATION

This type of modulation changes keys with no "notice," so to speak. The song just "jumps" from one key into the next. The most common form of direct modulation is from the old I chord to the new I chord, since this is the chord that establishes the key.

Try this example of Direct Modulation. The direct modulation happens in measure 7, where the piece "jumps" from D minor to A minor, and A minor becomes the new tonic.

PIVOT CHORD MODULATION

Another way to accomplish modulation is by use of *pivot chords*. Pivot chords lead smoothly from the one key into the another, avoiding the more jarring jump into the new key, as in a direct modulation. These are chords that have dual functions—one in the old key and one in the new key. Their dual functions are indicated by two analysis symbols (Roman numerals); one in parentheses showing the function in the original key, and one illustrating the function in the new key.

Try the following example incorporating a pivot chord modulation. Note that the modulation occurs at the second ending where the G chord stops functioning as ♭VII of A, and becomes ♭III in the new key of E Minor. Also, note that the left hand is played one octave below what is written.

Note the *tremolo* markings in the final bar. Rapidly alternate between the notes.

GROOVIN' TUESDAY

Track 38

The following pieces use modulations. Learn them for inspiration: then see if you can compose
your own pieces using this technique.

BELIEVE

Track 39

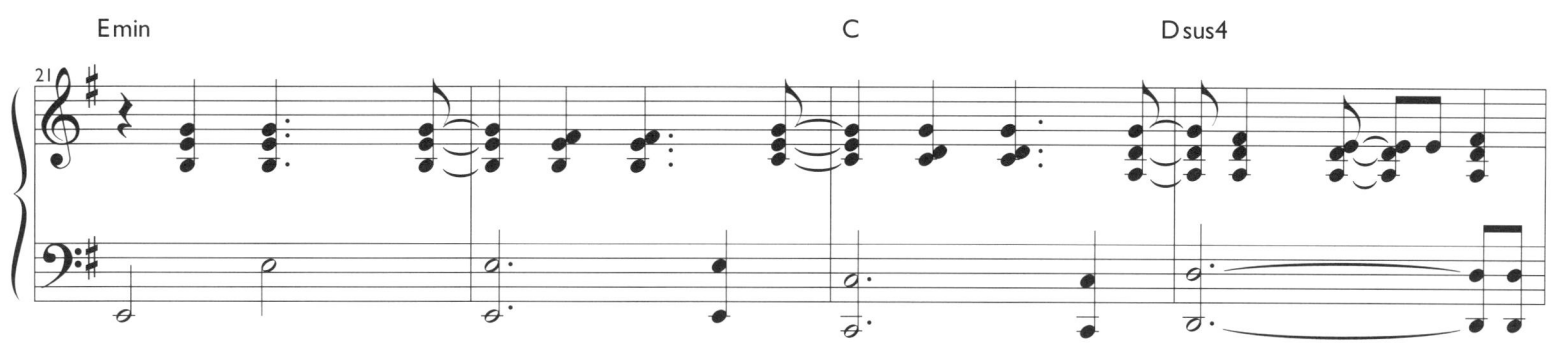

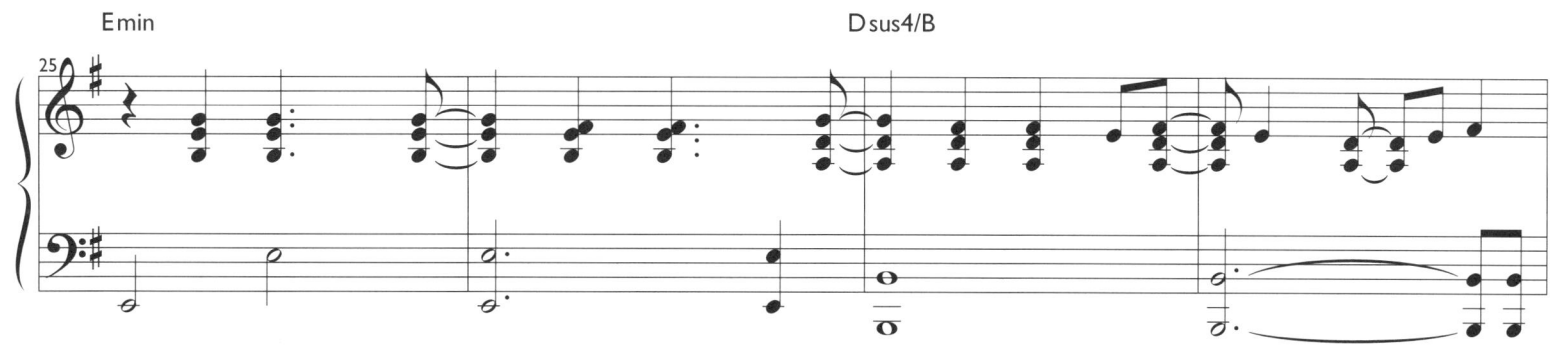

HOPE

Track 40

♩ = 120

CHAPTER 7

Rhythm and Groove

A keyboard player often has a supporting role in ensemble situations. Although we spend a lot of time focusing on the keyboard as a feature instrument, in reality that is often not the case. This chapter will focus on supporting parts—the keyboard as part of the rhythm section.

More often than not, if you are part of an original rock band, you will be expected to "jam" along with the rhythm section. That means you will come up with your own parts "on the fly," and probably never play the same part twice in a given tune. Typically, the type of parts you will see in this chapter would never be written out for you. At most, you may be given a chord chart. As your songs become more complex, or more arranged, you may then find yourself writing out specific parts for them. But usually, you will find you are needed more for texture, and will comp chords and play fills in an attempt to blend with the rest of the rhythm section.

The next few pages are classic examples of jammin' keyboard parts. Some good jam bands are Deep Purple, The Doors, The Allman Brothers, Phish and Aquarium Rescue Unit. Listen to them and even play along with the CDs. There is no better way to learn to play like them!

Remember, the following tunes give you great examples of how to back up a band and propel the groove.

A SHORT TUNA

Track 41

This example is in the style of Deep Purple's *Lazy*. It's a basic twelve-bar blues. This keyboard part should work with an organ sound as well as a piano sound, so give both a try if you can.

LACKADAISICAL

Track 42

Here is an example in the style of Aquarium Rescue Unit's *Satisfaction Guaranteed*. This should also work as either an organ part or a piano part. Notice the gliss in measure 16. Just slide your hand, or the nail side of the thumb, downward over the white keys.

NEVER SATISFIED

Track 43

This is a rock keyboard book but, just for fun, let's jazz it up a bit. Here is a rhythm part in the style of Ben Folds Five's *One Angry Dwarf*. Notice the use of major 7 chords, extensions and a more complex chord progression. Again, you would probably never see a part like this written out for you. This is the type of part you would come up with on your own while jamming with your band.

ONE ANGRY LITTLE GUY
Track 44

Here is an example in the style of Ben Folds Five's *Selfless, Cold and Composed*.

Track 45

HEARTLESSLY DECOMPOSED

The following example was written in the style of Ben Folds Five's *Song For the Dumped.*

FIVE FOLD EJECTION

Track 46

Stevie Wonder *was a Motown child prodigy who hit the top of the charts with* Fingertips (Pt. 2) *in 1963. He later matured into one of the most influential artists of the 20th century, recording most of the instruments on his dazzling solo albums.*

Let's take this rhythm thing one step further and get funky. Stevie Wonder is amazing at this type of thing. He has a lot of blues/jazz elements in his keyboard parts, and has mastered laying down the groove as well. Some of his parts jam, but some are also very specific to an arrangement, which means they would never change. The pieces in the last four pages of this chapter are in his style. Have some fun with them. Get some of Stevie Wonder's albums to hear how his parts fit into the arrangements. *Dream* is in the style of *I Wish*. If you're using an electronic keyboard, try an electric piano sound.

 *DREAM*

Track 47

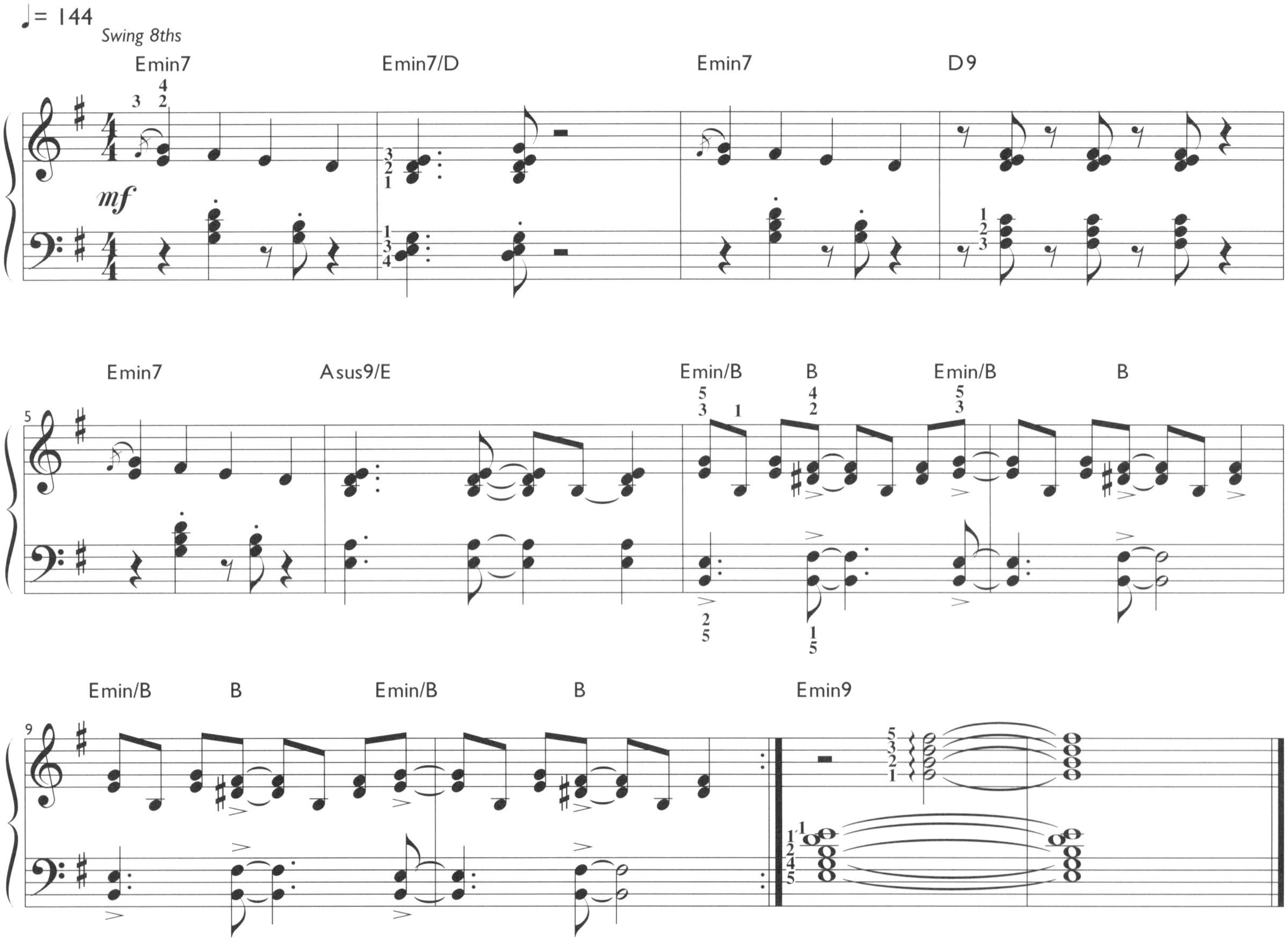

Here is a tune in the style of Stevie Wonder's *Superstition*. It is a good example of how Stevie Wonder lays down the groove with his left hand. If you have a synthesizer, try using a clavichord sound.

SUSPICION
Track 48

Chapter 7—Rhythm and Groove **67**

The following example is in the style of Stevie Wonder's *Boogie Reggae Woman*. Try using a synth piano sound.

BOOGIE DOWN & REGGAE

This last rhythm example is in the style of Stevie Wonder's *Higher Ground*. If you have a synthesizer, use a clavichord sound. Note that the right hand is notated in bass clef.

HIGH UP

Track 50

CHAPTER 8

Odd Meter

Odd meter encompasses time signatures that are not typically used or heard. Since most commercial music is written in standard meters, such as $\frac{4}{4}$, $\frac{3}{4}$, $\frac{6}{8}$, etc., the atypical number of beats per measure found in odd meter time signatures throws a rhythmic "curve ball" at the listener.

There are many odd meter time signatures, but in this book we will explore some more commonly used, such as: $\frac{5}{4}$, $\frac{5}{8}$, $\frac{7}{8}$ and $\frac{11}{8}$.

COUNTING AN ODD METER

Counting an odd meter can be tricky. The most commonly used method is *subdivision*. Subdividing is the method of breaking down each measure into smaller rhythmic groups according to how the measure is to be accented. Note that there can be more than one way to subdivide some odd meters.

$\frac{5}{8}$ TIME

Look at the following examples in $\frac{5}{8}$ (five beats per measure, the eighth note gets one beat). In example 38, beats 1 and 3 are accented. Therefore, the measure is broken into one group of two eighth notes and one group of three eighth notes, with the accent on the first note of each group. Also, instead of counting to "5" for each measure, each subdivision is counted separately (1-2, 1-2-3). Example 39 shows another subdivision.

Try clapping and counting the following two examples aloud. Be sure to clap the accents and count the subdivisions.

Beats 1 and 3 Accented (1,2 – 1,2,3)

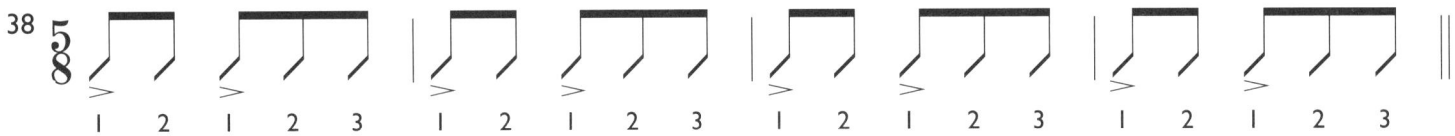

Beats 1 and 4 Accented (1,2,3 – 1,2)

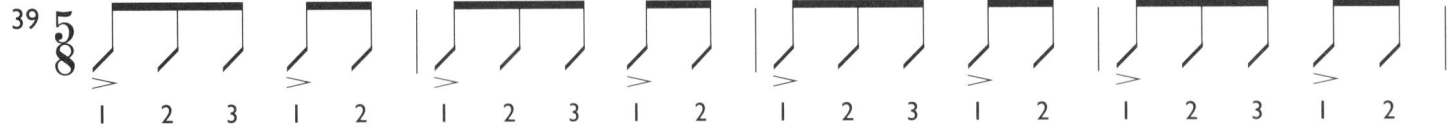

Try playing Examples 40 and 41 repeatedly to get used to how $\frac{5}{8}$ "feels." Chords have been suggested, but you can use any chord you like. Remember to count the subdivisions!

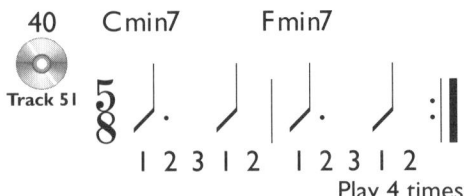

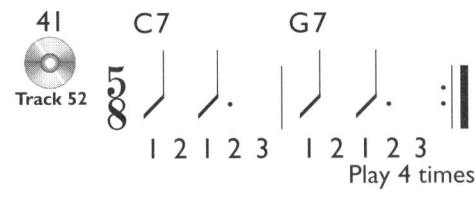

Here are some more examples of odd meters with some possible subdivisions. Pick any note or chord or use the suggested chords and try playing these rhythms while counting the subdivisions to get used to how they sound. Be sure to play the accents and count the subdivisions aloud.

 **$\frac{7}{8}$ TIME**

In $\frac{7}{8}$ there are seven beats per measure and the eighth note gets one beat.

Beats 1, 3 and 5 Accented (1,2 - 1,2 - 1,2,3) Beats 1, 4 and 6 Accented (1,2,3 - 1,2 - 1,2)

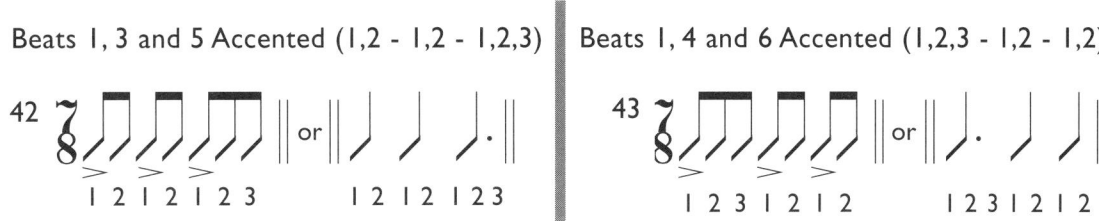

The measures in Example 44 alternate the way they are subdivided.

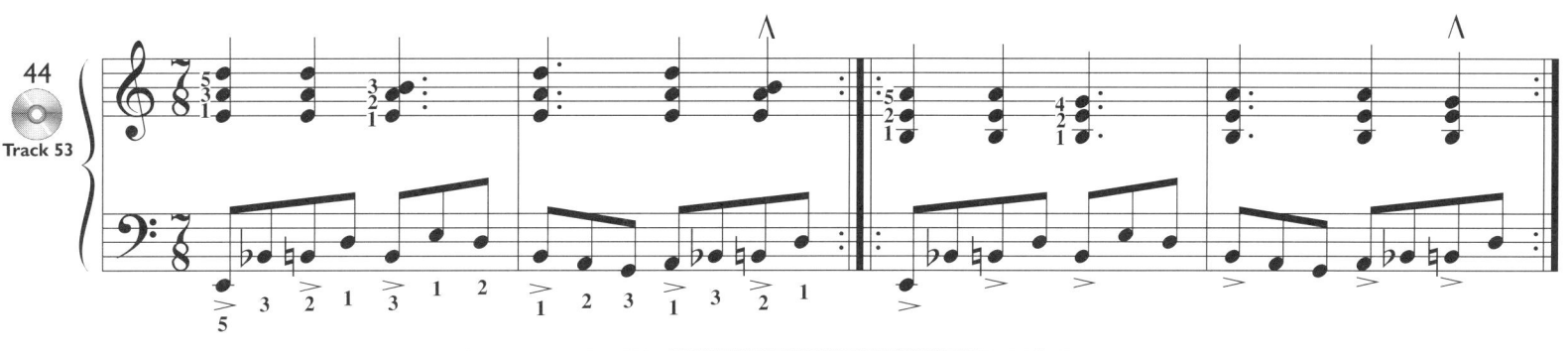

$\frac{5}{4}$ TIME

In $\frac{5}{4}$ there are five beats per measure and a quarter note gets one beat. You can still subdivide with eighth notes if you like. Example 45 uses a subdivision other than quarter notes.

Beats 1, 2, 3 and the "&" of 4 Accented (with eighth notes: 1,2,- 1,2, - 1,2,3, - 1,2,3)

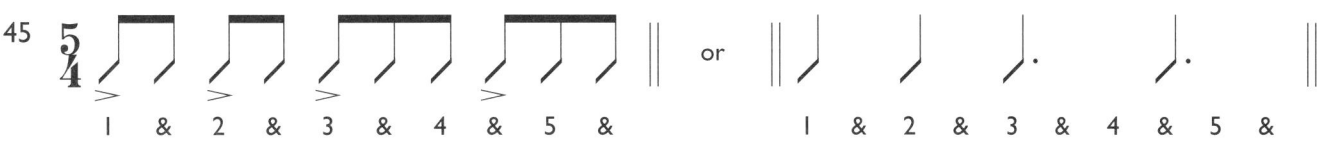

$\frac{11}{8}$ TIME

In $\frac{11}{8}$ there are eleven beats per measure and an eighth note gets one beat.

Beats 1, 4, 7 and 10 Accented (1,2,3 - 1,2,3, - 1,2,3, - 1,2)

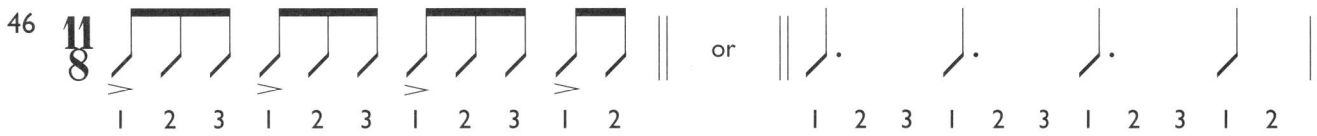

ALTERNATING TIME SIGNATURES

Here's an example of $\frac{5}{8}$ alternating with $\frac{7}{8}$. There are an endless number of possible combinations.

A good example of this rhythm can be found in *Distant Early Warning* by Rush, on their "Grace Under Pressure" album.

Star Kiss is in $\frac{5}{4}$ and is in the style of *Tarkus* by Emerson, Lake & Palmer. Notice the ostinato (see page 50) in the left hand (bass). Focus on coordinating the accents with both hands. Ready or not, you're in the land of odd meters, where anything can happen!

STAR KISS

Track 54

Simile = Continue to perform in the same style.

This one is in $\frac{5}{8}$. Note the counting pattern as indicated by the accents: 1,2, - 1,2,3.

JOY OF EXPECTANCY

Track 55

This one is also in $\frac{5}{8}$, but the subdivision pattern varies from phrase to phrase. Notice the use of parallel 4ths to cause dissonance and tension. Give special attention to where the hands cross (measures 7 through 9 and 15 through 20).

TIKI AND THE SQUEE
Track 56

Take a deep breath and relax. This isn't as bad as it looks. The time signature changes from measure to measure, phrase to phrase, but the eighth-note pulse remains constant. Just concentrate and count the subdivisions. Watch the tempo—it changes in measure 11. Notice that when the bass part is not included in the keyboard part, it is shown in parentheses. If you want to hear more of this kind of thing, the band Rush is notorious for alternating time signatures in their music.

HURRY

This piece is an extension of Example 44 on page 71. It has the same feel, the right hand starts with the same chord pattern and there is an ostinato in the bass. Think of this as an ensemble piece and your solo begins in measure 13. At that point, you can quit playing the written bass part if you like—the bass player can pick it up. Comp with chords in the left hand. If you have two keyboards, play sustained chords in the same register as your solo. It'll sound great!

RUMORS

Track 58

This tune is in $\frac{11}{8}$. Pay special attention to the interaction of the hands during the last six measures. **Enjoy!**

DANCE OF THE SILHOUETTES

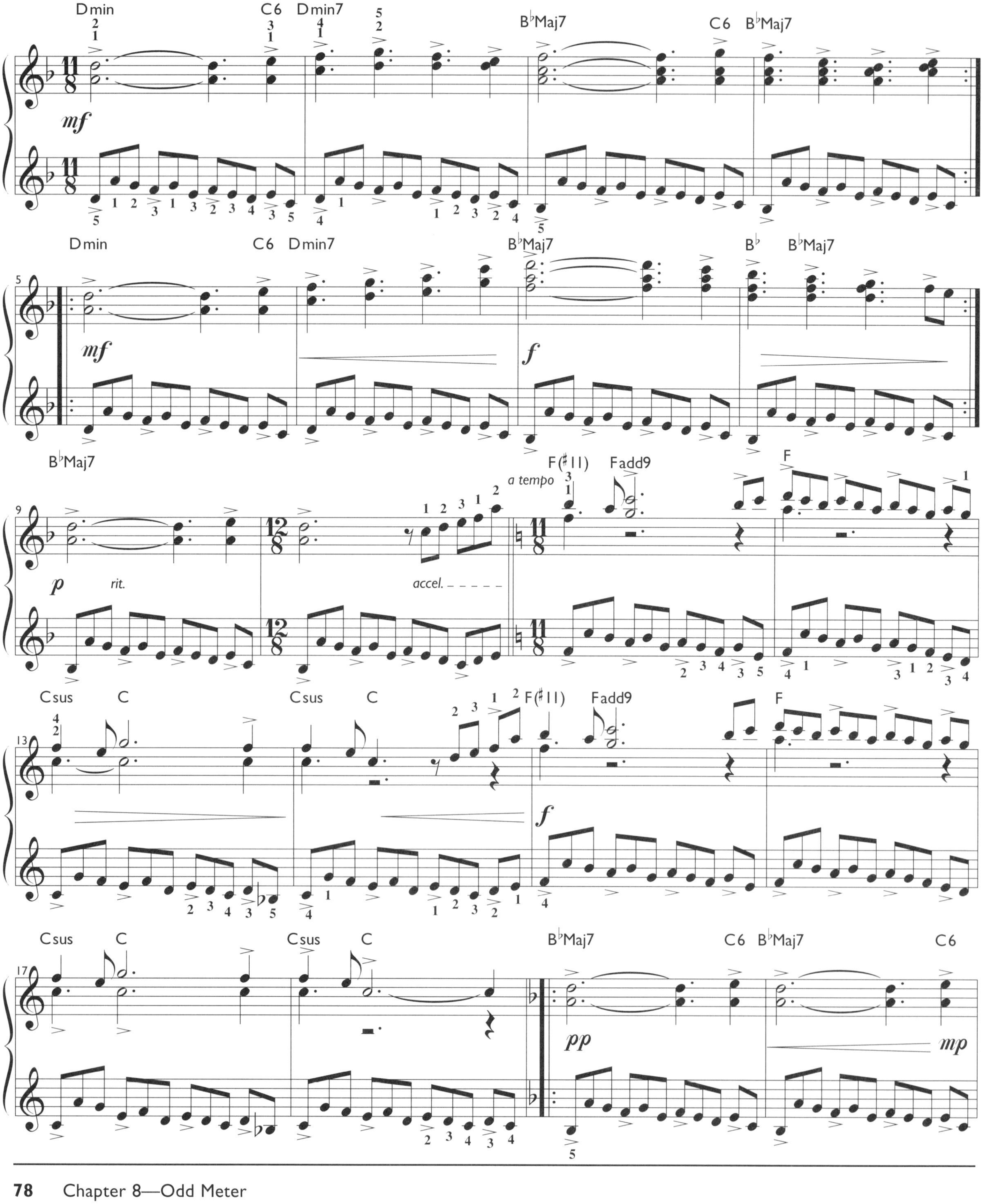

CHAPTER 9

Progressive Rock

Progressive rock evolved in the late 1960s and early '70s. It was an era where musical virtuosos brought elements of their classical and jazz backgrounds together with modern sounds, textures and grooves. Also, as we discussed in Chapter 7, there is a vast use of odd meter in progressive rock. This style of music is exceptionally exciting to the rock keyboardist because of the challenging parts and featured role the keyboard has in the ensemble.

Popular progressive rock keyboard sounds were, of course, piano and organ. But the 1960s and '70s were the decades of analog synthesis (pre-Korg, Kurtzweil, Roland, etc.). The sweet sounds of Moogs, Melatrons, Oberheims and ARPs can be heard in early progressive rock recordings as well as Hammond B3 organs with Leslie speakers. If you do not know these classic keyboards and how they sound, you should check them out.

In this chapter, we will explore the styles of the early generation progressive rockers. This includes groups such as Yes, Emerson Lake and Palmer (ELP), Genesis and Rush, as well as a couple of the new generation "prog" rockers: Dream Theater and Jens Johansson.

PHOTO • CHUCK PULIN\COURTESY OF STAR FILES, INC.

Keith Emerson's virtuosic, ground-breaking work with his trio, Emerson, Lake and Palmer, was a powerful fusion of rock and classical styles. This group was at the forefront of the British progressive rock movement in the 1970s.

Geddy Lee is a keyboardist and bassist for Rush. This band was a huge influence in the progressive rock movement of the 1970s and '80s.

Let's start by taking a look at some examples in the style of Rush. Rush's use of keyboards was more thematic and "part" oriented. Although Rush didn't have a "shredding" keyboard player in the band, they were a huge influence in the progressive rock movement. This was in part because of their constant use of odd meters, not to mention all of the vintage synthesizers that were such an integral part of their overall sound.

Here is an example of a moog part in the style of Rush's *Tom Sawyer*.

RIVER RUN

Track 60

Sub-Plots is in the style of Rush's Subdivisions, which has what is probably the closest they ever came to a keyboard solo. Try using a synth with a solid string sound and a quick attack time.

SUB-PLOTS

Track 61

Now let's take a look at some examples in the style of Genesis and keyboardist, Tony Banks. Tony Banks may be more of a team player than any other of the prog rock keyboard giants. Most of the brilliance of his work lies in his "playing for the song." His great use of texture and Romantic era classical music influences (Tchaikovsky) made the Genesis sound what it was. He did solo in many tunes, but his solos were more composed than improvised. None-the-less, he did great work. Let's take a look at his style.

Here is a moog solo in the style of *In the Cage*. There's no left-hand part because it's unlikely a keyboard player would ever have to accompany this kind of solo themselves. Notice the thematic development as well as harmonic development within this solo. If you don't have a mini moog, try to find a moog sound on your synthesizer. Even playing this on your piano should give you some insights into this great style.

OUT OF THE BOX

Track 62

Monday Matinee is in the style of Genesis's *Cinema Show*. This is also a great example of thematic development, as well as a practical application of counterpoint. Notice how the melody that begins in the right hand (measures 1 - 12), accompanied by the left, ends up in the left hand, accompanied by the right (measures 25 - 32). Whether the melody is in the right or left hand, be sure it is featured. If you're playing a synth, a fat string sound with a quick attack time works here.

MONDAY MATINEE

Track 63

Our last look at Genesis and Tony Banks is at a piano part in the style of *Firth of Fifth*. As you learn this, listen for the classical influence.

FIRST OF FIVE

Track 64

Let's take a look at the style of Yes keyboard virtuoso, Rick Wakeman. He is a classically trained pianist who developed a taste (not to mention talent) for blues and jazz, as a probable result of his pre-Yes studio session work. Legend has it that, as a student at the Royal Academy of Music in London, he used to sneak out, against school policy, to make extra money playing on studio sessions.

The following example is in the style of one of the Moog solos from *The Revealing Science of God,* which is twenty-nine minutes long. The extensive use of trills exemplifies Wakeman's classical influence.

Trills are notated as follows:

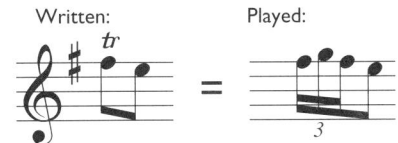

FORCES OF HEAVEN

Track 65

PHOTO • CHUCK PULIN/COURTESY OF STAR FILES, INC.

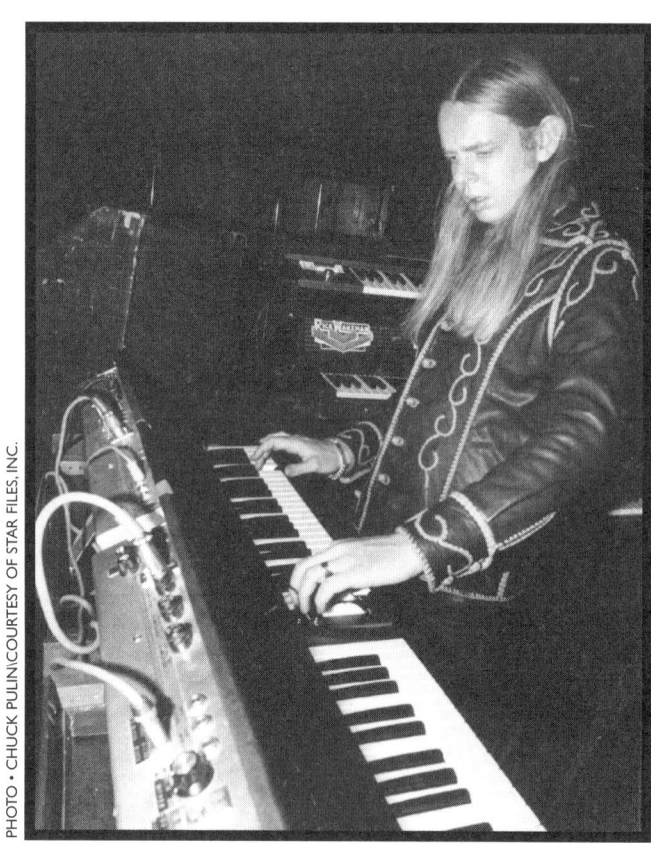

Rick Wakeman *joined Yes in 1971, introducing multiple keyboards, such as mellotron, clavinet and harpsichord, to the group's sound. He quickly became the focal point of the band's live performances.*

Wake Up also demonstrates Wakeman's classical influences. It is in the style of the piano part in *Catherine of Aragon* from his solo album, "The Seven Wives of Henry VIII."

WAKE UP

Track 66

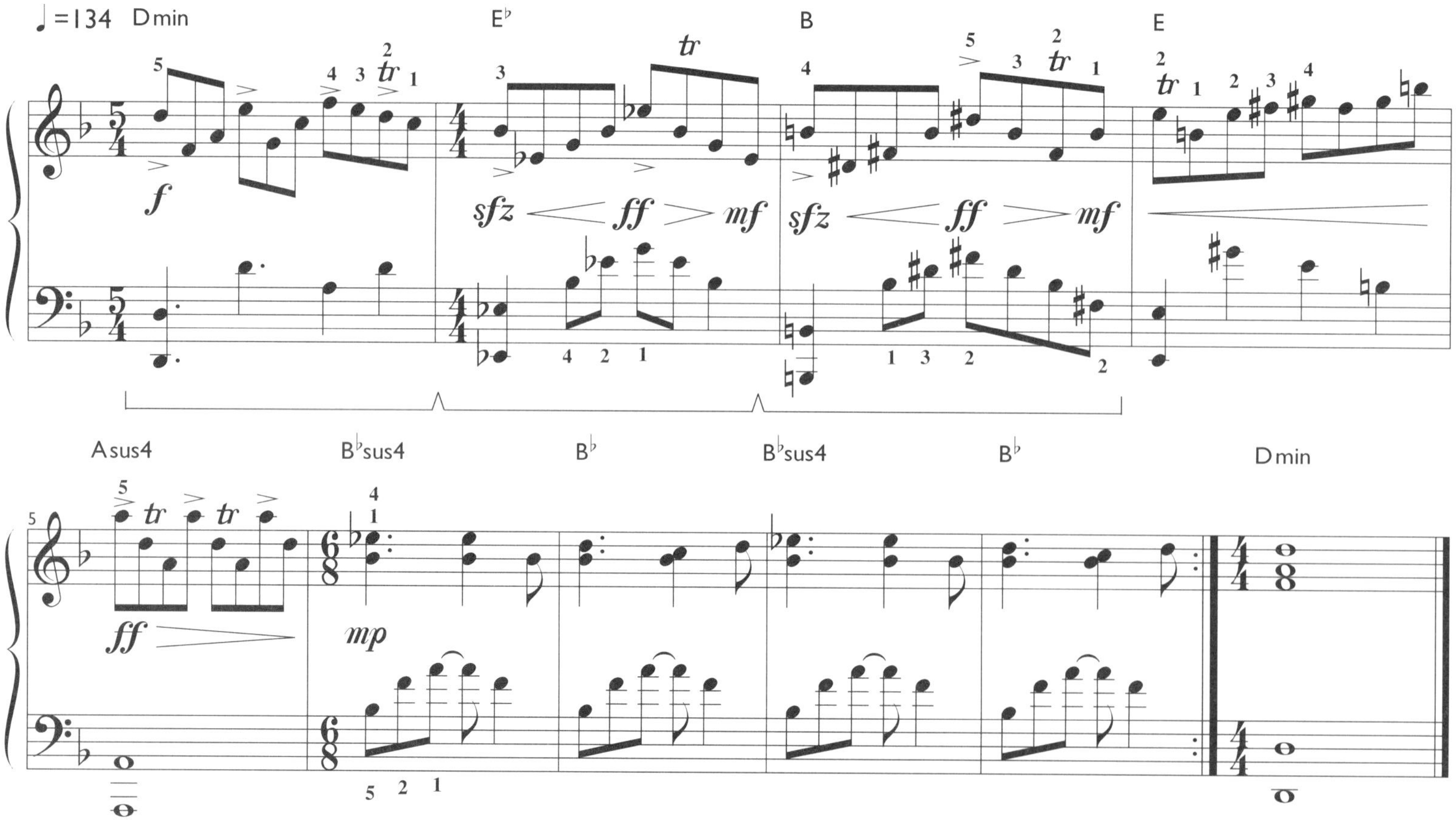

Here is a bluesy organ solo in the style of *Roundabout*.

AROUND AND ABOUT

Track 67

Let's take a look at the style of Keith Emerson of ELP. Emerson is probably the most harmonically advanced rock player of his generation. He is greatly influenced by more modern classical music (Stravinsky, Bartok and Mussorgsky). He sometimes arranges entire pieces of classical music, such as Mussorgsky's mighty orchestral work, *Pictures At An Exhibition*. The dissonance and use of parallel harmonies in these composers' works are also apparent in the music of Keith Emerson. The chromaticism and wild improvisation found in jazz also plays an important role in his soloing style.

Destined Chance is in the style of the moog solo in *Lucky Man*. Note that this piece is *monophonic* (the moog is a monophonic instrument, meaning it can only play one note at a time). Watch the clef changes; the solo jumps back and forth between the bass and treble clefs, although it can be played entirely with the right hand.

DESTINED CHANCE
Track 68

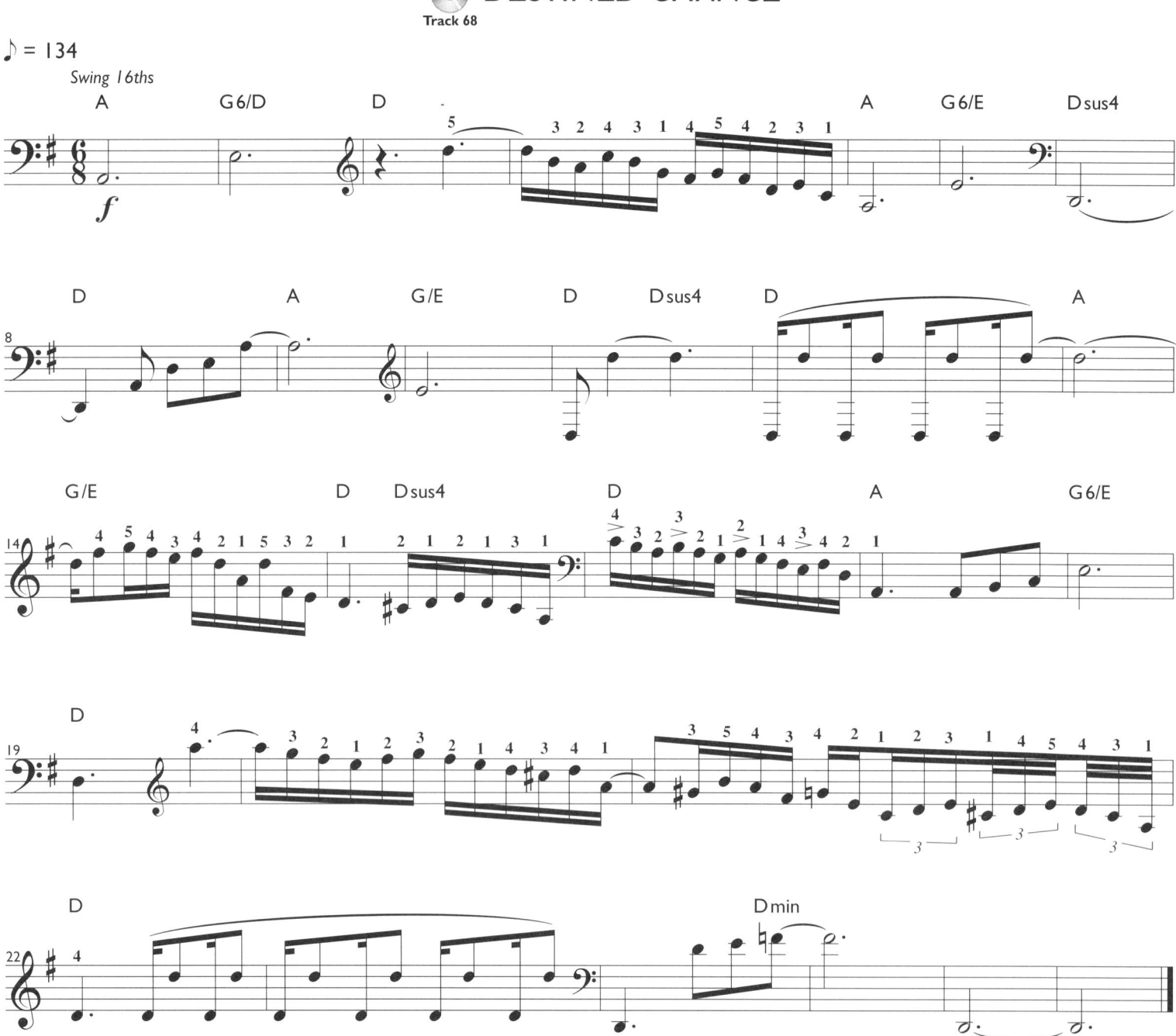

Carnival is a jam in A♭ Dorian, in the style of an organ solo in *Karn Evil 9*, an ELP classic.

CARNIVAL

One of Emerson's most impressive performances was his arrangement of *Toccata* by the Argentinian composer, Alberto Ginastera, who himself praised the arrangement. This is a great example of Emerson's ability to translate contemporary classical music influences into rock arrangements. Here's a tune in the style of Emerson/Ginastera:

REGATTA

Let's jump ahead to the late 1980s and '90s. The next example is in the style of Dream Theater, probably the most popular prog rock band of the late '90s. All the band members are amazing musicians, especially the keyboard player, Kevin Moore. Their music is influenced by all of the classic bands, especially Rush. *Nightmare City*, in F♯ Mixolydian, is in the style of *Metropolis*. Notice the use of chromaticism. Although F♯ is not the key of choice for us keyboard players, get used to it because guitar players love it. Again, it's unlikely a keyboard player would ever have to accompany this kind of solo in the left hand, so only a right hand part is shown.

NIGHTMARE CITY

Track 71

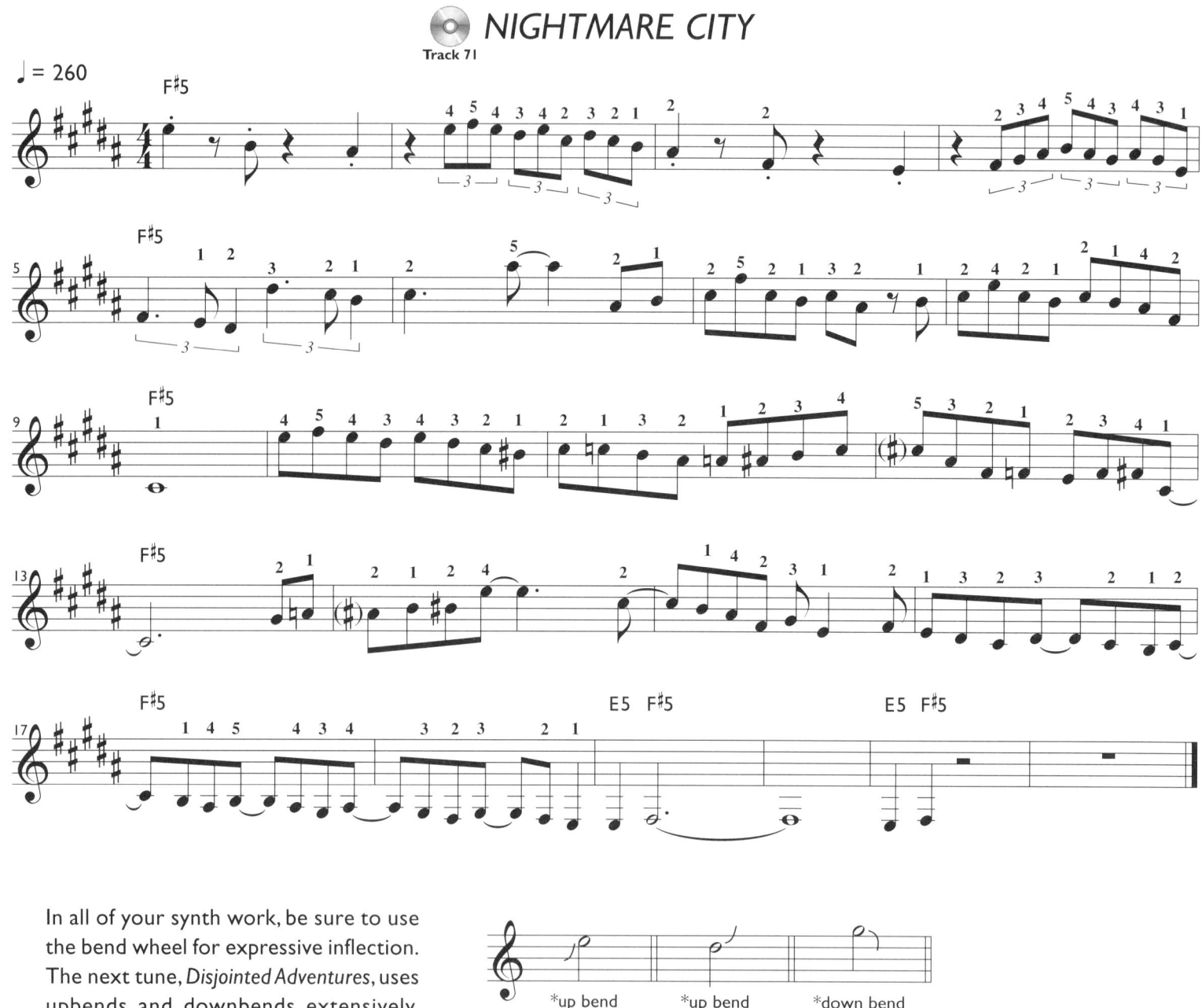

In all of your synth work, be sure to use the bend wheel for expressive inflection. The next tune, *Disjointed Adventures*, uses upbends and downbends extensively. Pay attention to these markings.

*up bend before note   *up bend after note   *down bend after note

> **Note:**
> Bend wheel can be set on most synths in half-steps from 1 to 24. Experiment with different settings. This next piece works well with a setting of 2.

Finally, this tune is in the style of Jens Johansson. Although he isn't a member of a specific progressive rock band, he is an amazing player. He has worked with guitarists such as Yngwie Malmsteen and Alan Holdsworth. This next example is in the style of *Joint Ventures* from the "Heavy Machinery" album he did with Alan Holdsworth. This sounds best with a synth brass sound. If you're looking for inspiration, check out this album.

DISJOINTED ADVENTURES

Track 72

While this is the end of this book, it isn't the end of the story. To continue building your rock chops, study classical and jazz music and any other kind of music you can get your hands on. Keep on learning!